YouthBuild's North Star

YouthBuild's North Star

A Vision of Greater Potential

Second edition

John Bell

2013

YouthBuild USA • 58 Day Street, Somerville, MA 02144 • (617) 623-9900
www.YouthBuild.org

ISBN: 978-0-9916524-0-2

Contents

Foreword

John Bell has been a key communicator of the most important ideas in the YouthBuild movement for the past 25 years. He has orchestrated staff trainings, conferences, fellowships, and academies. He was the architect of YouthBuild USA's training capacity and leadership development work. He has developed systems of teaching in our conferences based on the most interactive methods of learning. John has kept our eyes on the prize, built learning communities, and written several handbooks for YouthBuild as well as key articles that have been widely used in the youth development field. He has consistently put forth an impassioned view of the role of leadership development and liberation from oppression as fundamental to YouthBuild's success. I believe there is no YouthBuild director, staff, or graduate, or YouthBuild USA staff who has not been directly or indirectly influenced by his wisdom and knowledge, whether they are aware of it or not.

This book is a generous gift to all of us from John. Nobody asked him to write it; nobody funded it; nobody set aside time in his schedule of work to put his ideas together in this impassioned and inspiring way. He wrote it on his vacations and weekends. He deeply desires to have all YouthBuild programs implement the biggest vision, the most impactful design, the most powerful philosophy of social change.

His passionate and skillful, well-organized and visionary, driving and graceful contribution to YouthBuild since 1978 has played a key role in its success and its integrity. He has been my YouthBuild partner as well as my life partner. I have infinite gratitude to him.

Please know that although YouthBuild as such started in 1978, its roots are deep in the civil rights movement, as both John and I arrived in New York City in the 1960s as activists inspired by the leadership of that movement. We had each embedded ourselves as teachers in different community-controlled schools in Harlem before we even met. Our paths were destined to cross, and they did on the weekend after the murder of Martin Luther King Jr.

Please join me in thanking John for the gift of this book, the gift of love and perseverance, of vision and determination to use our collective effort to make a better world for all people everywhere through the creation of a positive force of young leaders emerging from the YouthBuild movement all over the world.

Dorothy Stoneman
November 2013

Preface

THE MAIN POINTS OF THIS BOOK

At its core, YouthBuild's founding and guiding "North Star" is to be part of a broad social justice movement aimed at eliminating poverty and creating a "beloved community," to use Dr. Martin Luther King Jr.'s image, in which all humans have the opportunity to flourish. One of YouthBuild's main contributions to this effort is the development of young leaders who are skilled and inspired to work to realize this vision. To accelerate the development of these young leaders, and to deepen YouthBuild's impact in the world, in this book I propose that there are six interdependent strands of the YouthBuild model that need deepening or improving:

1. Build on current practice to prepare young people increasingly well for college, postsecondary learning, and careers as building blocks for successful, satisfying, and sustainable lives.

2. Place leadership development in a central place in YouthBuild and align the program to promote young leaders.

3. Foster critical learning that equips young people with an understanding of the economic, political, and social situation in which

we live, and helps them develop a vision for a just society and pathways to get there.

4. Deepen the healing process so that young people can shed their past hurts and unworkable habits that hold back their leadership, learning, love, and liberation.

5. Build an even stronger positive peer culture that models the way we want the world to be, provides ongoing support to make the hard individual changes needed, and becomes the new reference point and network for future growth.

6. Sustain a vibrant graduate-leadership and alumni-support program that provides training, skill development, leadership opportunities, and public-policy roles that strengthen their leadership and impacts the wider world.

ORGANIZATION OF THIS BOOK

This book is written for the YouthBuild community—directors, staff, boards, students, graduates, YouthBuild USA, our funders and supporters. This is a vision, not a how-to book. There are excellent handbooks available for each current YouthBuild component that detail the best practices and resources for implementing a YouthBuild program. My intention here is to build on those resources, and to offer my best thinking for the future development of YouthBuild, based on the values, experience, observations, practices, and principles that have guided my work in YouthBuild for decades. Each of the chapters spells out my vision for the main parts of a YouthBuild program. Near the beginning, chapter 3 lays out a holistic picture of what a bold, fully developed, well-integrated transformational YouthBuild program might look like. The next two chapters explore the importance of being clear on the program's core values as a guide for forming the program's core values, design, and culture (chapter 4), and building a strong, cohesive staff (chapter 5). Chapters 6 through 10 sketch out what each of the five YouthBuild program components (leadership development, education, counseling and healing, construction, and graduate resources) would look like if they were aligned with the "North Star" of leadership development towards transformation of society. Chapter 11 draws a picture of YouthBuild USA's national graduate leaders network, past, present, and future. The final chapter briefly restates the case for emphasizing the development of leaders and recaps four key strategies addressed in the book.

For online readers, there are hyperlinks sprinkled throughout the book that will lead you to resources relevant to the current topic. These include articles, PowerPoint presentations, facilitator's guides, handbooks, and websites of organizations mentioned in the book. For readers of the hard copy, references to these resources are listed in the resources section in the back of the book.

A HOPE AND A DEDICATION

It is my hope that the vision of YouthBuild's North Star put forth in this book will offer inspiration, higher aspirations, a future direction, a reference point, or a stepping-off point for your own good thinking. A vision, by definition, is not reality. As you read parts of this book, you may have the inclination to dismiss it as unrealistic, idealistic, or pie-in-the-sky. But before dismissing the idea, you might ask yourself these questions: *Do I like this idea, even if it seems impossible? Would I like to see YouthBuild be more like this? If so, where does my resistance come from? Am I giving in to my own accumulated sense of powerlessness? Have I somehow settled for too little? What would have to change in me to embrace more of this vision? What external resources or capacity would be needed to make this a reality? What individual role could I play?* On this last question, you might like to remember Margaret Mead's famous quote: "Never doubt that a small group of thoughtful, committed, citizens can change the world. Indeed, it is the only thing that ever has."

I honor the sustained caring and hard work of YouthBuild staff, directors, graduates, and YouthBuild USA staff who over the years have made such a difference for untold numbers of people. It is not just the 130,000 young people who were in YouthBuild between 1994 and the completion of this book in 2013. It is also the ripples that have gone out from them to the perhaps millions of family members, friends, and colleagues who have been positively impacted by what the YouthBuild students and graduates gained from their YouthBuild experience. The vision put forth in the following pages flows from and stands on the solid foundation built by the dedicated YouthBuild staff, participants, and graduates who have gone before. This book is a deep bow of gratitude to them, and a call to take YouthBuild to the next level of transformation—a hope that I believe lies deep in our hearts.

In addition, I would like to appreciate some specific individuals who contributed to the ideas in this book. First and foremost is Dorothy Stoneman, my lifelong partner and founder and CEO of YouthBuild USA. Even after more than 40 years of marriage and working together, she continues to inspire me with her commitment, caring, consistency, and courage. She has often been called a force of nature. Her boundless energy and idealism fuels the movement; her wisdom about how to build this movement has informed all of our progress; and her indomitable faith in humanity's possibilities has deeply impacted my life and is reflected throughout this book. I have been blessed beyond measure to be her partner.

I want to thank the numerous people who took the time to read drafts of the book and give me critical feedback, specific edits, and important challenges to consider. Sue McCammon, wife and partner of former YouthBuild director Bob McCammon; YouthBuild graduate leaders Noe Orgaz and Joel Miranda; YouthBuild directors Suzanne Fitzgerald, Anthony Hubbard, Derek Steward, Jennifer Lawrence, Eliska Champagne-Veselka, and David Clauss; and YouthBuild USA senior staff Charlotte Richie, Sangeeta Tyagi, Monica Zeno-Martin, Helen Whitcher, Daryl Wright, and Scott Emerick. And, of course, Dorothy

Stoneman, who, as my editor in chief, read successive drafts, argued me out of some of my more extravagant ideas, and kept me grounded in the possible.

Their contributions made this a better book. I am deeply grateful to them all, not only for their help with the book but for their years of commitment to the YouthBuild movement.

1

The Door

*T*hey came in for good reasons. Maybe they were lost and wanted to find their way back. Maybe they were suffering and needed healing. Maybe they had just had a child and realized they needed to get serious. Maybe they aimed to flip the script of their lives and become somebody admirable. Maybe they knew they were smarter than their school records or more caring than their criminal records or more capable than their work records. Maybe they were required by a judge to enroll. Maybe they were sick of a messed up world and wanted to help change it.

When they arrived at the door each was met with respect and kindness. Each was listened to deeply about their journey and why they wanted to come here. Out there, they were treated as undeserving people, assumed to be worthless. In contrast, in here they were told that they were sacred beings, worthy of love and respect, to be treated with caring and compassion, patience and faith. They were also told that they had to want to be here, that it was not easy, that much would be asked of them, that they would have to be self-disciplined and courageous, that they would have to keep at it even when they didn't feel like it. This was a hero's journey, not for the faint of heart. They were capable of great things, even beyond their imagination, but it would not be handed to them; they would have to work hard, with no guarantees. They would have to make and re-make their own decision to be here.

If they decided to come, they would find a welcoming and safe place—a community of like-minded people; a positive, encouraging culture. They would find people who believed in them, didn't hold their pasts against them, and would be there when things got tough. They would be expected to learn their ABCs and learn to love learning itself; they would be expected to be a leader here in everyday things, and gradually to serve the community and take responsibility for ever larger circles out into the wide world. They would be expected to learn how to love and be loved, how to accept and show caring and appreciation, how to cultivate compassion and forgiveness. And they would be expected to face their inner demons, and to liberate themselves from limiting beliefs, old fears, and unworkable habits. They would be assisted and expected to create healthy practices for their bodies, minds, hearts, and spirits.

They would be asked to explore questions like *Who am I?*, *What is my purpose in life?*, *What am I called to do?*, *What are my gifts and talents?* They would be told: *You are not just someone who needs help getting your schooling, or getting a job, or getting ahead, or getting yours. It's about not settling for a small vision; it's about rising up to who you really are, and daring to realize the dream of a just and human society. So much is possible for you, if you believe it and if you work for it. Are you ready for this? The door is open.*

2

YouthBuild's North Star: What and Why

Since YouthBuild's federally authorized funding first reached local communities in 1994, through 2013, over 130,000 young adults walked through the doors of YouthBuild. There are currently 10,000 young adults ages 16 to 24 in YouthBuild programs throughout the United States at any given time. These young adults are smart, talented, and want to make a difference. At the same time, the world is in serious trouble. Our environment, economy, and communities are hurting. The original vision of YouthBuild was to bring these two elements together—unleashing the power and intelligence of young people to tackle the enormous problems of the day. This is what I call YouthBuild's "North Star," its guiding light, its navigational compass, its symbolic reference pointing to transformation.

YouthBuild is not primarily a job training program, although it does provide job training. YouthBuild is not primarily a high school completion or college-prep program, although it does offer high school completion and college prep. YouthBuild is not primarily a builder of affordable housing, although it does train students to build affordable housing. YouthBuild is not primarily a life skills program, although it does teach life skills. For most part YouthBuild does all these things well. But many other good programs offer these services. So what is YouthBuild's niche?

YouthBuild was conceived and launched back in 1978 as a movement-building effort to reduce poverty and extreme inequality, and to expand opportunity for all people to realize their full potentials. From the movement's beginning, young people shared decisions with adults and developed their leadership roles, while rebuilding their own lives and positive future prospects.

YouthBuild is developing a tremendous resource of skilled, motivated, and caring young leaders for helping to solve the world's problems. But there are several things in our current version of YouthBuild that need to change in order to fully unleash that resource. YouthBuild has achieved amazing success in providing conditions for thousands of young people to transform their lives, and has had measurable positive impact on many other youth-serving networks and policies. All true. At the same time, I believe YouthBuild has far greater potential influence and depth to offer. My intention is to paint a picture of that potential in these pages. The door scene in the opening chapter is part of that picture. The greater potential starts from the moment a young person comes through the door; it starts with setting out the expectations and asking each person to make a decision. Our vision is also part of that greater potential. It means keeping the long range mission of YouthBuild clearly in view—that we are part of a long struggle for individual achievement in the context of building a decent society. This is another feature of YouthBuild's North Star.

PAST AND CURRENT SUCCESS OF YOUTHBUILD

For over 30 years, I have been proud and privileged to serve Youth-Build in many capacities, from founding staff member of the first YouthBuild program to a vice president of YouthBuild USA. In that time YouthBuild has achieved notable successes as measured by external data and research, the internal growth and transformation of tens of thousands of young people, the tangible assets of affordable housing we have produced, and the extraordinary international demand for YouthBuild that has grown since 2001.

The data tell the following story of growth and impact. Beginning in 1978 with just one program in East Harlem, New York, by 2013 Youth-Build had:

- Expanded to 273 programs in the nation's poorest communities, involving 130,000 young people in building over 22,000 units of affordable housing

- Secured 1.3 billion dollars of federal funding, and significant support from many of the largest private foundations and corporations

- Created a voluntary, democratic affiliated network of 216 programs

- Developed 55 diploma-granting schools, including 34 charter schools

- Incorporated ten state YouthBuild coalitions charged with advocating for state funds

- Instituted a robust array of graduate leaders councils and initiatives.

We have honed such a comprehensive program model that other systems now want to learn from and partner with YouthBuild. Because YouthBuild has worked successfully with adjudicated youth, resulting in a recidivism rate that is forty percentage points lower than the national average of 67 percent, YouthBuild has received funding from the criminal justice system to run demonstration projects as an alternative to incarceration or re-entry programs. Because YouthBuild takes in high school dropouts and produces high school graduates bound for college, the public education system increasingly recognizes and funds YouthBuild as charter and diploma-granting schools.

Because YouthBuild is adopting green building practices, the trade unions are partnering with us because we are well-situated to provide pre-apprenticeship–level workers for the emerging green industry. Through the YouthBuild AmeriCorps program, which engages disadvantaged young adults in providing significant service to their communities, YouthBuild has demonstrated that the national-service agenda should include low-income populations in giving service, not just receiving it. Finally, other national nonprofits are coming to us to learn how we managed to get and hold a line item for funding in the federal budget.

Then there are the thousands of young people, represented in this book by Antonio Ramirez, Antoine Bennett, Natalia Diaz, and Mike Dean. These are four young people with whom, a few years ago, most people in the country would have avoided contact. According to their own reports, they were involved in various negative activities, sometimes including gang activity, street violence, or drug dealing. They were among the 3.5 million young people in the United States, ages 16 to 24, who are out of school, out of work, and raised in poverty. As Dorothy Stoneman, founder and CEO of YouthBuild USA, often says, this group of human beings has been dismissed by society—disregarded, discriminated against, and disrespected in numerous ways. Consequently, these youth have become disillusioned, disheartened, discouraged, disgusted, discontent, destructive, despairing, and disengaged. The nation calls them disconnected, for short, because they are not connected to education or employment. The young people call themselves "dissed."

But these young people want the same things all people want—they want to know their true nature; they want to provide for themselves and their families; they want to make a contribution to their communities; they want to feel happy and safe.

Fortunately, Antonio, Antoine, Natalia, and Mike found their way to YouthBuild and transformed their lives. You would be pleased to have them as neighbors and coworkers. They have contributed to transforming their communities.

Antonio Ramirez is from Rockford, Illinois. One Halloween night, he was cruising the streets when his best friend, riding next to him, was shot and killed. After struggling with his impulse for revenge, he knew he had to find a way out of the street life. He found his way to YouthBuild, which nurtured his innate leadership qualities. Ten years later, he served as branch director of youth programs for the YMCA in Rockford, serves on the board of several community organizations including his own YouthBuild program and the national board of YouthBuild USA, has a beautiful family of a wife and three children, and owns his own home. A few years ago, the city of Rockford selected him one of the 40 most outstanding community leaders under age 40. Now he is involved in bringing YouthBuild to Mexico (the country of his ancestors), and El Salvador, and is starting his own consulting non-profit for youth development.

Before YouthBuild, **Antoine Bennett** was incarcerated for 18 months for committing a violent crime. Since YouthBuild, he has become the executive director of his own job-training and positive-fatherhood program in Baltimore, owns his own home, and is a community leader. Along with Antonio, he serves on the board of directors of YouthBuild USA. He says, "I used to be a menace to my community. Now I'm a minister to it."

Natalia Diaz, daughter of a Salvadoran immigrant and raised in Washington, DC, had been sucked into vicious gang life as early as age 12, was in and out of jail, used and sold drugs, and was pregnant and homeless at 16. Now, some years later, she works as a guidance counselor for youth and families, and is enrolled in college. She has two wonderful, healthy children.

Mike Dean says,

> I never had an easy year growing up in Columbus, Ohio. I lived in a drug-infested home without a father. My neighborhood was drowned in confusion and negativity. The lack of positive goals and dreams led me to a life of crime. I dropped out of high school with a baby on the way. I had no home, no money, and no help. I put my hope into crime and the streets. At that time, it seemed that this was my only option. Crime and the streets eventually led me to jail. I came close to death on multiple occasions. The loss that changed everything was the tragic and violent death of my younger brother .

That was 1997. He entered YouthBuild. Today Mike is program director of his local YouthBuild program, a minister of his own church, owner of his own construction company and his own home, and is happily living with his wife and four children.

To be realistic: Most young people who enter YouthBuild come there to get their GED, a little money in their pockets, and some job preparation. They don't usually declare up front that they want transform their lives or be a community leader. Some do not rise to the leadership opportunities. Some do the bare minimum to get by. Some have learning or emotional disabilities that inhibit their growth. Some take years to get their lives on a positive track, after the seeds nurtured by YouthBuild have ripened. But the majority of young people are open to real transformation if the conditions are right. Just under the surface of profound conditioning to settle for little, to feel powerless, or to "get mine" lies a deep sense of unfairness and a deep yearning for a decent life for everybody. Our job as YouthBuild staff is twofold: to take the long view about a person's human potential, and to create the conditions that accelerate the realization of it. This yearning is what YouthBuild reliably unleashes.

Because of these conditions, tens of thousands of young people like Antonio, Antoine, Natalia, and Mike have transformed their lives through YouthBuild. Roughly half have achieved their GED or high school diploma while in the program, and many more after the program. Roughly half also have found immediate placements in jobs, careers, or postsecondary education. An increasing number are entering college and persisting to credentials. Seventy percent of Youth-Build students have registered to vote, and, in one study, the majority of graduates reported that they do vote. In the same study, the students' own estimate of their life expectancies increased by 32 years. The list below describing some positive life outcomes is from *Life After YouthBuild: 900 YouthBuild Graduates Reflect on Their Lives, Dreams, and Experiences*, by Andrew Hahn et al.

Success highlights of graduates

- 74.6% are currently working, going to school, and/or in job training
- 76.2% are free of government supports and not receiving food stamps, welfare payments, or unemployment benefits
- 85% have some involvement with the community
- 92% have positive attitudes
- 80% are free of negative behaviors

Source: Life After YouthBuild: 900 YouthBuild Graduates Reflect on Their Lives, Dreams, and Experiences *(Andrew Hahn et al; Brandeis and Temple Universities, 2004)*

And the story doesn't stop there! Because of YouthBuild's successes in this country, like-minded social entrepreneurs in other parts of the world have discovered YouthBuild. In 2013, as many as 102 Youth-Build programs are operating in 13 other countries including South Africa, Mexico, Brazil, Israel, Serbia, Haiti, Jamaica, Honduras, Nicaragua, Costa Rica, and El Salvador, and expanding to more countries every year.

THE POTENTIAL OF YOUTHBUILD IS EVEN GREATER

This level of success and influence is amazing, and we could rest here, knowing we had done well. I sometimes reflect with awe and gratitude at how much has been accomplished. Thousands of caring, dedicated YouthBuild staff have devoted tens of thousands of person-years toward the well-being of the young people. My heart is full of love for them. And yet, as someone intimately close to YouthBuild over its existence and as someone with a tendency to think long-range, I believe that YouthBuild is still in the early stages of its development, and that its potential transformational impact is just emerging. For example, just in the last five or six years we have been learning how to set up programs to expect graduates to go to college, build affordable green housing, create pre-apprenticeship pathways to green industries, engage volunteer mentors to support young people through the program and the transition into responsible adulthood. YouthBuild directors and staff are making inspiring innovations, and new kinds of community partnerships are blossoming all over the YouthBuild network.

Building on current trends, what picture of YouthBuild's future might emerge? Here are some questions we might ask ourselves that point in the direction of YouthBuild at its fullest expression. Most of this has been tried at various times by some local programs, but hasn't become standard practice:

1. What if we always viewed YouthBuild as essentially a youth leadership-development process at its core, aimed at promoting community change agents? How would that shift our curriculum, our emphasis, our opportunities, and our culture? What if staff were hired as leadership developers, with specialties in teaching, construction, counseling, career development, program management, and so on?

2. What if we reconceived YouthBuild not as a nine- to twelve-month full-time *program* but as a life-altering transformational *process*

that integrated many different ways for young adults to engage, for as long as needed? What would that look like? How would we convince funders to support it? How would that shift our programming, recruitment, staffing, and performance objectives?

3. What if we consistently expanded education beyond the classroom and deliberately viewed the entire program as a deep learning environment? How would that shift our operations? What if construction staff were explicitly considered teachers and counselors?

4. What if all across the YouthBuild network, we engaged students, whether in GED or high school diploma track, in deep learning, critical thinking, or project-based, inquiry-oriented learning relevant to their real lives? What if we had a GED or high school diploma curriculum that explored leadership development, people's histories, cultural competencies and issues, community organizing, responsibility to their communities, and making a difference?

5. What if we knew how to go deep with students on their emotional healing so that their traumas, dramas, and irrational habits did not sabotage their lives? What if we had the expertise on staff to go beyond crisis management to help young people deal with their early developmental issues like basic trust, ability to form lasting relationships, self-love and confidence, and so on? What if we provided students with tools for forming healthy relationships and effective parenting? What if we taught young people methods of peer counseling so they can help each other and themselves without an official counselor? What if these methods could become lifelong tools?

6. What if YouthBuild International's work offered opportunities for staff and student exchanges for leadership development and culture exchange? How could we fund this? How might international travel and learning accelerate youth development? What if

an international experience was a standard part of a YouthBuild experience?

7. What if we could develop nearly self-sustaining sources of revenue to help diminish YouthBuild's reliance on federal funding and allow the movement or program more flexibility? How could we position ourselves as schools for local and state average daily attendance (ADA) public-education funds even more than we are now doing? How could we develop revenue-generating enterprises that could employ some of our graduates and plow back earnings into the program? Green construction and retrofitting services? Housing development, sales, or rental? Running a day-care center or training students to run family day-care centers? Home nursing services and IT services for YouthBuild programs with those training tracks? And so on.

8. What if a local YouthBuild program positioned itself as a premier social-justice or community-organizing center, serving the community with meeting space, policy initiatives, community organizing campaigns, and leadership development? Furthermore, what if each local YouthBuild program was putting out a similar set of principles and public-policy recommendations, such as those listed in the *Declaration of Inter-Dependence,* a policy statement by YouthBuild graduates voicing their ideas for positive change, that other local YouthBuild programs around the country were sharing, that had been worked out through a democratic process of the Affiliated Network?

9. What if, furthermore, our graduates were supported not only to further their educations, to secure steady, sustainable work lives, and attend to their families and children, but also, as the time ripens, to run for elective office—for school committee, community planning board, union leadership, city council, state government? As part of our mission, what if we viewed our role as intentionally

and deliberately developing the next general of community activists and leaders?

10. What if we consistently viewed YouthBuild as developing a prototype model for what Martin Luther King Jr. called "the beloved community"? How could we build out into the larger society what we have learned, and will learn, about community, caring, forgiveness, acceptance, positive culture, competence, success, communication, learning, cooperation, and change?

11. How do we maximize our public-private partnership with the federal and state agencies to create longevity and strong bipartisan political support because our outcomes are superb?

12. How would YouthBuild USA's role need to shift or expand to assist the YouthBuild field in doing all of the above?

UNCERTAIN TIMES REQUIRE CLEAR VISION, VALUES, AND INTENTION

These questions are not new to us. Someone in some YouthBuild program somewhere is doing or trying to do each or many of the above. The challenge ahead is to make these widespread. Those of us who have been around YouthBuild for a while want to move in these directions. There are four reasons for raising these questions about the future direction of YouthBuild at this time:

1. The inevitable need to transition away from Dorothy and John

Dorothy and I are nearing the end of our YouthBuild work.[1] We have no immediate plans of leaving YouthBuild, but our days ahead are cer-

---

1. For any reader not familiar with us, Dorothy Stoneman is the founder and CEO of YouthBuild USA, and I am a vice president of YouthBuild USA. Dorothy began the first YouthBuild in 1978, and I joined her then, left to be a political folk musician for a few years, and then returned full-time at the founding of YouthBuild USA. We have been married and partners since 1970 (43 years as of 2013).

tainly fewer than the days behind. So transition thinking is upon us as a practical reality. The values and vision that we have embedded into YouthBuild, both individually and collectively, will be passed on to those who take over our leadership roles. Those values and vision will no doubt change somewhat with new leadership. Given this, it makes me want to restate the founding values and vision clearly. That is one purpose of this book.

2. Uncertain political climate and federal funding expansion

YouthBuild's federal appropriation is contingent upon Congress and the executive branch, which are both ever-changing. We have always had to simultaneously plan for expansion and contraction, because politics are unpredictable. However, funding streams tend at best to be incremental, so even if the climate of cutting spending and reluctance to raise taxes changes, we can't depend on YouthBuild seeing a huge federal expansion, although it would certainly be appropriate. There is potential for state YouthBuild funding, but this is still subject to changing political and economic priorities. Given these conditions, how does YouthBuild expand its influence and impact?

3. Federal funding—a mixed bag

Without federal funding, the expansion of YouthBuild would be even more incremental, with local programs depending on local, state, and private dollars to mount a typical $700,000 annual operation for only 35 young people. Indeed, the two primary reasons that Dorothy Stoneman chose the route of federal funding for YouthBuild back in 1988 are: it was apparent that only the federal government had this level of resources; and, she believes, it is the responsibility of government to see that all its citizens have adequate education, job opportunities, and affordable housing.

Federal funding has fueled the spread of YouthBuild and the development of the YouthBuild model far and wide. However, when the government runs YouthBuild as a federal grant program, there are understandable constraints, and programs must meet the performance objectives of the government. For the first 13 years, the federal Youth-Build appropriation was administered by the U.S. Department of Housing and Urban Development (HUD). The HUD YouthBuild program was oriented toward housing development and partnering with neighborhood agencies working for community economic development. In 2007 the federal YouthBuild program was transferred to the U.S. Department of Labor (DOL). The DOL YouthBuild program is oriented toward preparing young people for the workforce and post-secondary placements.

The agendas of the government agencies have had the helpful effect of focusing or refocusing attention of the grantees on the required outcomes. But these funder focuses can also divert the practice of YouthBuild away from the original leadership development intent that inspired YouthBuild in the first place, with the power of love and respect as the guiding method. Leadership development is specifically written into the authorizing law, and DOL is embracing it. Nonetheless, constant attention to truly implementing leadership development is needed, lest it get sidelined by DOL's emphasis on placements and certifications.

4. Distracted by its own success. Too many opportunities.

As noted above, various systems, organizations, government agencies, private foundations, and corporations want to be involved with Youth-Build. At its own initiative, YouthBuild has deliberately pursued opportunities to expand its reach and effectiveness in areas such as mentoring, green businesses, state criminal justice funding, energy efficiency, new career pathways, union partnerships, charter school development, rural economic policy work, and international work. Corporations increasingly see YouthBuild as a way to promote their charitable agendas. These opportunities (or threats) will likely increase in the future as YouthBuild becomes even better known. YouthBuild may be seen variously as a recruiting ground, a market, a public relations boon, a beneficial partnership, a way to solve a major problem, and so on. To sift through various opportunities, our values and vision need to be clear so that the tail does not end up wagging the dog. So far, so good. But this is worth keeping an eye on.

A SHORT BIOGRAPHY

To give you a glimpse of what shapes my values and vision as it informs YouthBuild, I want to share some broad themes of my background. I was raised working class in the small, naval shipyard town of Bremerton, Washington, near Seattle. Catholic boyhood, parents both Democrats. Hardworking neighbors who were auto mechanics, floor tilers, road pavers—most of them were also alcoholics, alcohol being the drug of choice to deal with hard times.

My father dropped out of high school during the Depression to support his parents, and was a soldier in World War II, during which he met and married my mother, who was working as a nurse. Discharged from the army in 1945, he took the photography skills he had learned in the army and opened a little studio. But Kodak cameras were on the rise, diminishing the need for a family photographer. He didn't cope well, and became an alcoholic.

My father was kind and humorous when sober, but angry, bitter, or maudlin when drunk. He would go to work in the morning, and either come home drunk or would start drinking as soon as he got home at night. To my young boy mind, all I knew was that something out there was hurting my dad. And since I saw the same thing happen day after day to most other fathers around the neighborhood, I made a decision in my early adolescence that somehow I was going to help change the world so that it was better for my father and people like him. I didn't have understanding then of what I would later come to know as economic class oppression, compounded by racism and sexism, but I knew something was wrong.

Then the 1960s hit. I was 16 to 26 years old in the 60s—my formative period of high school, college, and young adulthood. I was radicalized by the assassinations of the Kennedys; Martin Luther King Jr.; Malcolm X; Schwerner, Chaney, and Goodwin; and Medger Evers. I participated in the civil rights and anti-Vietnam War movements, and was schooled by Karl Marx, Mohandas Gandhi, Paulo Freire, Ivan Illich, Franz Fanon, Marcus Garvey, Malcolm X, Martin Luther King Jr., and other radical thinkers of the 60s. (Dorothy and I met at a church gathering of movement activists on the Sunday after MLK Jr. was killed.)

Throughout the late 1960s and the 1970s, I helped organize protests and actions, walked in picket lines and stood in silent witness at peace vigils. These included times of being tear-gassed, arrested, and briefly jailed. From 1967 to 1973, I worked in community-controlled alternative schools and freedom schools in Harlem and East Harlem. I lived on 137th Street in Harlem for 15 years, worked in communities of color since 1967, and have learned through much personal experience about the toll of white racism on the lives of people of color and on the humanity of white people. Additionally, for eight years, from 1984–92, I was a founding staff member of an international youth leadership program called Children of War, which brought young victims of war and oppression from 18 different war zones to tell their stories and mobilize young people in the United States to take action. This deepened my understanding of worldwide conditions that hurt and oppress people, especially young people.

Dorothy Stoneman had also come out of the ferment of the 1960s, active in the civil rights and anti-Vietnam War movements. We married in 1974 and formalized both our personal and our political partnership, which has continued strong to this day. Dorothy and I lived in Harlem from 1970 to 1985. We had been teachers in schools in Harlem and East Harlem, and for us it was important to be part of the community in which we taught. Neither of the political parties was doing much for the people we knew and loved in our community. So, also in 1974, Dorothy, as the key conceptualizer and leader, myself, and some friends started what we expected to become a political party. We called it the "New Action Party for a Human Society."

Dorothy wrote a set of party papers, one of which was a 50-year plan to take political power! You might be thinking, *Sure, you and who else's army?!* True, most of the progressive young people in my generation saw the abuses of power and wanted nothing to do with it. So some "tuned in, turned on, and dropped out" and others built alternative programs and movements inside the system. But those of us in the New Action Party believed that if you wanted serious, fundamental change, then you had to have power. We also believed that we had to do something big and concrete if the party was to gain support. People needed to say, *Those people know what they are doing, and they do it well.*

So our 50-year plan proposed that there be a central action program addressing one of the five key areas we had identified for social change—an action program that would be able to gain the support of a huge majority of people. One of these was the tragic situation for low-income young people. We had come out of education and freedom schools. We knew that everyone supports the development of youth. We also knew that young people had an inherent sense of injustice and latent idealism, even if they had been silenced or suppressed by the weight of institutions and oppression. So we went to young people we had known when we taught them in elementary school, and asked them what they would do to improve their communities if they had some money and adult backup. Young people always have good ideas. The adult world often doesn't listen. We did.

And so, with Dorothy in the lead, we started the Youth Action Program as a youth-initiated and youth-implemented leadership-development and community organizing project. We intended to build a youth movement to succeed the one that Dorothy and I had been part of in the 1960s. YouthBuild grew straight out of that. (And I might point out that as of this moment, in 2013, we are only 35 years into our 50-year plan!)

MY ROLES IN YOUTHBUILD

I was the first YouthBuild counselor, from 1978 to 1981, teaching young people, at their request, a method of peer counseling that I was trained in so that they could effectively help each other with their emotional issues. I then began a short-lived career as a performing folk musician, singing about the same social issues I had been working on, but adding the beauty and poetry of music. I rejoined the YouthBuild effort in 1988, when we formed YouthBuild USA as the national support center for an emerging YouthBuild network. Since then I have had a chance to lead and manage a wide variety of projects and program initiatives, including leadership development, mentoring, diversity, counseling and healing arts, and environmental awareness. I have developed innovative training and technical assistance formats like the Directors Fellows, the Diversity Working Group, the Academy for Transformation, and the Leadership Development Learning Communities. In recent years I have had the great good fortune to lead our graduate leadership work. These leadership roles have given me perspective on YouthBuild that is deep and broad.

3

Current Mission and Future Vision of YouthBuild

MISSION OF YOUTHBUILD

The mission of YouthBuild is to unleash the intelligence and positive energy of low-income youth to rebuild their communities and their lives. YouthBuild seeks to join with others to help build a movement toward a more just society in which respect, love, responsibility, and cooperation are the dominant unifying values, and sufficient opportunities are available for all people in all communities to fulfill their own potential and contribute to the well-being of others.

This is the up-front mission found on YouthBuild USA's website. It is a powerful statement with huge implications. This is what I will be calling YouthBuild's "North Star" throughout this book. What does it mean to "rebuild their lives and their communities"? What does it mean to "help build a movement toward a just society"? How would YouthBuild need to counteract the deep cynicism and despair about changing things that make it look like young people today don't care about anything beyond themselves? What would YouthBuild look like at the fullest expression of this mission, if we kept the YouthBuild North Star directly in front of us as the guide?

A BROAD VISION FOR YOUTHBUILD

Using this mission statement as a stepping-off point, I want to sketch my vision of YouthBuild as a mature and well-developed realization of that mission sometime in the future. Most of these concepts are not new. Creative and hard-working YouthBuild directors and staff have already developed many of these elements to one degree or another. Other elements are already well-established. But as a holistic, completed, widely implemented picture, it is ahead of us.

There will be thousands of local YouthBuild programs in every kind of low-income community. These programs will be recognizable by their practice of overarching principles that include caring and the power of love coupled with the power of opportunity, cemented by the emphasis on education and the development of youth as leaders. The main vocational focus of these programs will be construction-based projects, though several other occupation areas will have been developed, especially in the fields of renewable energy, environmental clean-up, information technology, and health care. Hundreds of graduates will become YouthBuild staff and directors. With some exceptions, each YouthBuild program will be implemented under one roof, with all the components integrated by a cohesive staff that collectively buys into the mission and creates a caring, competent context for the participants.

YouthBuild will be a multiyear transformational process rather than a nine- to twelve-month program. Holding to the mission of YouthBuild as a force for community transformation from the onset, YouthBuild will be implemented as a long-term process of developing leaders that has many phases. There may be a pre-YouthBuild phase for young people who may not be quite ready for YouthBuild, either emotionally or academically. The pre-YouthBuild phase will allow these young people to connect with a positive leadership program and prepare academically or behaviorally to succeed in a full-time Youth-Build program. The second phase will be what is currently considered the YouthBuild program, that is, it will be full-time and paid, and offer skills training, academic classes, leadership training and opportunities, counseling, community service, career development, and graduation. The third phase will be a robust, fully funded graduate support phase that includes transition to full-time employment, registered apprenticeships, or college outside the program. Graduates may keep a strong continuing connection to YouthBuild as long as they want to through career support, counseling, organized community service, leadership activities, political study groups and actions, and social activities. Thousands of YouthBuild graduates will be attending college, supported by YouthBuild USA's solid Postsecondary Education Initiative (PSE) work already being implemented across the YouthBuild network. Phase three will be flexible enough to attract and accommodate graduates at whatever level of time and interest they have. The third phase will have a staff and a budget. It will be a center of community and political activity, and learning. It will present new challenges as well as support, which will continue that "family feeling" graduates may have had while in the program phase of Youth-Build. The case for the effectiveness and cost-benefits of this extended conception of YouthBuild will have been made and accepted by public and private funders.

YouthBuild will be a household name that garners widespread support from the community, corporations, governments, foundations, individuals, and the media. Creative advertising on TV, magazines, and billboards will have made "YouthBuild" a cherished brand name.

Untold numbers of YouthBuild graduates will be playing leadership roles in the wider community. YouthBuild will be seen as an effective citizenship education program, developing people who have vision, ethics, and skills, and understand the political and legislative processes. YouthBuild graduates will be staff in community organizations, running for local, statewide, and national political office, involved in the local schools, on community planning boards, or other public sector work, and so on.

YouthBuild's reputation as an educational leader will be cemented. YouthBuild programs will be widely viewed as successful alternative schools, many of which will be public charter schools. YouthBuild programs will send a majority of their former high school dropouts—now high school graduates—on to college, registered apprenticeships, and postsecondary learning. YouthBuild's approach to the education of formerly disconnected youth will be recognized as so successful that YouthBuild principals and teachers will be consulting with the local boards of education. Perhaps YouthBuild USA will become a source of training for public-school principals. The approach will combine critical thinking, practical skills, project-based curricula, and the use of the whole community as a classroom. Emphasis on paths to higher education (from colleges and universities to trade schools to registered apprenticeships) and the motivation for lifelong learning have supplanted earning a high school equivalency diploma as a main education goal.

YouthBuild will be a recognized leader in the area of green construction of low-income housing and weatherization of existing housing. With the integration of green-building practices already well underway, YouthBuild students use the best of the latest environmentally sound construction materials and methods to produce affordable housing that is energy-efficient and cost-sustainable. The young people will earn industry-recognized certifications, and will be recruited in large numbers for careers in the burgeoning green-construction industries. Construction staff will also teach the young people about the connection of green building to the environmental crisis. In addition, YouthBuild graduates will be active as green educators and activists, alerting their own communities to the realities of global warming, climate change, and environment justice, and helping to organize local campaigns on green issues.

YouthBuild will be so effective as a crime-prevention approach that judges will consider it one of the best alternatives to incarceration, and federal and state governments will fund it as an alternative to sentencing or a re-entry program. Recidivism rates of Youth-Build students and graduates will remain radically lower than those of the general court-involved population. Adjudicated youth in Youth-Build will reliably turn their lives around in a positive direction. The most successful of these youth will be mentoring younger youth to help deter them from paths towards incarceration, advising community agencies about how to build healthier communities, and educating younger people and officials about the sources of and solutions for crime.

YouthBuild will be recognized as being very effective in the area of counseling and personal transformation. Over the years, Youth-Build will have developed an effective holistic approach to personal growth and development. The approach will include skilled therapy from caring counselors; the consistent use of groups to support personal growth; the systematic teaching and use of peer counseling to spread sources of support deeper into the program and for lasting use after graduation; and the use of Narcotics Anonymous, Alcoholics Anonymous, and other 12-step programs in communities where they are well done. Each program will have staff teams consisting of a counselor, teacher, and construction staff who care about the personal development of 10 to 15 participants, plus a referral network of outside agencies built on solid relationships. Social-emotional learning and health will be the lens through which all staff view the students. YouthBuild counselors will offer training to other YouthBuild staff on elements of effective counseling (like listening, confidentiality, boundaries, empathy, stress signs, and so on). Restorative practices will be the commonly used way discipline and conflict are handled. Youth-Build counselors will be consulting with public schools, social service agencies, probation departments, etc. on effective ways of counseling youth. Mentoring will be an integral part of each young person's experience. Soon after they begin, they will voluntarily choose a mentor who commits to at least a 15-month relationship. This relationship will extend into the graduate phase of YouthBuild and will assist with the transition to the postsecondary education and career stages of the graduates' development as well as their community-leadership roles.

YouthBuild will be looked to by the wider community for help in dealing with cultural identity issues and tensions. Over the years, YouthBuild programs will have successfully developed healthy ways to handle issues of race, gender, sexual orientation, class, and other identities. When divisions around race or ethnicity emerge, YouthBuild will be turned to as an organization that has a useful and coherent set of ideas that help people make sense of the world, helpful processes of healing emotional wounds, strategies of handling everyday oppression more effectively, methods of bridging divisive attitudes and prejudices, and pathways to getting people organized in the efforts to eliminate injustice. Both staff and graduates will be playing leadership roles in exploring issues and forging alliances for change and community among conflicting groups.

YouthBuild will have always recognized the need to address the emotional and spiritual well-being of its members. Beyond teaching students basic construction skills, life skills, and adult-education skills, YouthBuild programs in the future will be providing students and staff alike ways of handling stress, doing emotional healing, and acknowledging a life of the spirit in nondenominational ways. At YouthBuild, people will be able to learn things like meditation, yoga, 12-step methods, mindfulness, peer counseling, stress-reduction techniques, and support-group processes.

Job placement of YouthBuild graduates will be easy because employers will recognize the quality of worker that YouthBuild produces. Graduates will be well-trained, have good work habits, know how to cooperate with other employees, and have good attendance and productivity. YouthBuild will have a sophisticated job-readiness approach that weaves together a sector analysis of the local job market, superb training of the young people, personalized and institutionalized relations with local employers, on-the-job support and mentoring of graduates, and strong relationships with trade unions that will provide construction-oriented graduates apprenticeship training en route to well-paying and substantive careers. YouthBuild programs will have employers standing in line committed to hire graduates.

YouthBuild will provide young people a process of forming their own political analyses. It is helpful for people who have been subject to systematic oppression and misinformation to develop a coherent set of ideas or analysis about why things are the way they are, and what can be done to change them. In YouthBuild, young people will be exposed to various social and economic theories, and will be asked to probe the conditions of their own communities and ask *How did things get like this?* and *How can we improve them?* They will also be exposed to the thinking of leading social critics and leaders in the effort to help them form their own sets of ideas and visions for the future that help them get their bearings in a culture thoroughly saturated with a free-market framework of a corporate-consumer economy. They will use the curriculum *Blueprint for Democracy,* which was carefully created by YouthBuild USA to begin this discussion.

YouthBuild will be recognized as a model that encourages personal economic self-sufficiency. For example, many graduates will be running their own companies in the areas of construction, solar-panel installation, environmental clean-up, information technology, home day care, and health care. Many YouthBuild programs will have developed a for-profit business branch that hires graduates and continues to serve the community and whose profits support the basic YouthBuild program. Hundreds of YouthBuild graduates will be serving as YouthBuild staff across the nation. YouthBuild USA will be offering a national, proven solar-window installation franchise to local Youth-Build programs and graduates to run as a business.

YouthBuild will be noted for its long-term support of its graduates. Over the years, YouthBuild will have figured out how to develop deep follow-up programs of graduate services, alumni clubs, statewide and national connections, mentoring of younger people by older graduates, and ongoing leadership opportunities. For YouthBuild graduates, the idea of *Once in YouthBuild, always in YouthBuild* will be even more real, and comparable to traditional models of lifelong allegiances as exist in some sororities and fraternities. They can build on the hard-won growth they accomplished during the program phase. They can complete their high school equivalency diplomas if needed, continue their men's or women's support groups, get help with job interviews, continue tutoring the second graders in reading, get support for starting their own businesses, have mentors themselves, or join with other graduates to take action to change something in the community. Each local program will maintain robust social-networking media that connect graduates to each other and further resources. The graduate program could include the incubation of small businesses like day care, house painting, or construction companies. The overarching themes will be self-development, community development, and continued involvement in YouthBuild. Graduates will be engaging in community work in a deeper way, for example, by organizing youth conferences, getting active in their children's schools, being liaisons with other community organizations, running for office, and spearheading alumni initiatives for specific community issues. They will also participate in fundraising for their own programs and the national movement.

YouthBuild itself will be a center for community revitalization. Out of YouthBuild will flow ideas, leadership, and energy for improving communities. Increasingly, board members, directors, staff, and young people will sit on community boards and planning groups, lobby elected officials, organize voter-registration and turnout campaigns, propose community development projects, join and initiate coalitions, and lead collective impact collaboratives to tackle tough issues. Young people's leadership and involvement will always be supported. Youth-Build sponsoring organizations will make their facilities available as meeting spaces for community groups. In addition, YouthBuild itself, especially through its graduates, will be running additional programs for the wider community like after-school centers, mentoring programs, sports leagues, young entrepreneurs incubators, and so on. Of course, many of YouthBuild's sponsoring organizations have already been doing this before adopting YouthBuild as one of their elements of community development.

YouthBuild will be set up as an effective learning organization for all. Funds will be budgeted for generous staff-development opportunities and adequate pay and increases. Staff will be encouraged to take classes and trainings that enhance their work. Programs will be staffed to the efficient-maximum, not to the overwork-minimum practice supported by funders. Program design will allow for staff retreats for reflection on successes and obstacles, adequate vacations for recuperation, and sufficient breaks between cycles to evaluate the program and make desired changes. In addition, regional YouthBuild programs will have a menu of opportunities for cross-training and collaborative learning communities to share best practices.

Many local staff will have been certified by the YouthBuild USA Academy for Transformation. In the effort to achieve a higher level of consistency across YouthBuild programs and to deepen staff development, local staff will receive an intensive series of courses sponsored by YouthBuild USA. Counselors and teachers in particular can attend a monthlong training institute two summers in a row and receive graduate credit towards an advanced degree and become an official YouthBuild counselor (or teacher), with an accompanying pay increase, and influence on and recognition by the wider professional community.

The YouthBuild USA Affiliated Network and the national youth councils will be both a source of excellent program standards and

monitoring and a political force in state and national policy arenas. These arenas will include education, job and career training, youth employment, environment, criminal justice, national service, leadership development, diversity, rural and community development, and poverty alleviation. Its membership, legislative, and program-auditing committees will be well-functioning. Its governance structure will be strong and well supported by all, as it is today. (See the *YouthBuild Program Design and Performance Standards*.)

Nationally, YouthBuild will be playing a coordinating role with other key national organizations in forging a national program for social transformation that includes getting business, government, education, labor, grassroots, religious, and philanthropic sectors to agree to reconfigure the national mission away from maximizing the single bottom line to maximizing human well-being for all. Already active in this endeavor, YouthBuild will increasingly have representatives serving on state and national policy councils, a broader legislative agenda, articles and books written that will influence public awareness, and have its own TV show featuring YouthBuild young people, staff, and allies.

YouthBuild graduate leaders will represent YouthBuild's vision and mission even more powerfully and regularly at conferences and policy forums. A robust national graduate leaders network with high-functioning national councils (like the National Alumni Council, Young Leaders Council, PSE VOICES, National Speakers Bureau) already exists; in the future this network will include state centers of graduate support, training, leadership development, and policy work staffed by YouthBuild graduates.

As the number of non-US YouthBuild programs increases, there will be some version of a YouthBuild International Affiliated Network linking these programs, bringing leadership together for cross-cultural sharing, highlighting successes and best practices, and solving problems. Programs in many countries around the world have already adapted the YouthBuild model. Within these programs, there will be youth and staff leadership exchanges and work projects to open minds and make connections. There will be an International Young Leaders Council that will provide guidance and policy input to the international movement. Education for leadership will be the common thread, and young leaders will learn how to support each other across borders and will address issues related to creating a global youth movement for justice, peace, and a sustainable world. (For more information about our international work, see the YouthBuild International website, www.YouthBuildInternational.org.)

A FEW NOTES ON THIS VISION

In closing this section, I'd like to make four more comments about this future vision.

Vision is neither new nor complete. This vision is ambitious and far-reaching. For veterans of YouthBuild, most elements are not new. Some have been included in the YouthBuild USA Affiliated Network's *YouthBuild Program Design and Performance Standards* guide; others have been spelled out in Dorothy Stoneman's articles and in Youth-Build USA's handbooks. Many YouthBuild programs have created and developed pieces of this vision. And it is anchored YouthBuild's mission. But even if elements of it sound familiar, we are still a long way from realizing a holistic and widespread version of this vision. The task is to bring it to scale, so that it is consistently implemented across the field. Obstacles include lack of capacity, funding constraints, executive leadership focus that is diverted from deepening the movement to merely helping it survive, and an economic system that is not currently investing in the well-being of all its people.

Is it inspiring or daunting? For some YouthBuild staff, directors, and graduates, building towards this vision might be exciting and inspiring. For others, it might feel daunting and overwhelming. We all begin from where we are and move forward. Some of us have the energy to rise to the challenge of maximizing YouthBuild's greater potential. Some of us groan under the current weight of too little funding, inadequate staffing, or constraints of state education charters, and roll our eyes at the thought of doing even more towards a bigger vision. The beauty and power of the YouthBuild network is partly the vast diversity among us—the commonalities of caring and commitment that bind us together, and the various interpretations, inventiveness, experimentation, and innovation around the basic shared vision. The generous ways we share resources, best practices, and good ideas; the ways we cooperatively teach each other and bring each other along— these are reasons for hope in achieving a bigger vision.

Do not settle for too small a vision. Most of us settle for a life that is too small for us, one that doesn't come close to matching the depth of our aspirations to make a difference. Many, if not most, of us come to accept limiting notions that were drilled into us over a lifetime with messages like *You can't do it!* or *You can't fight city hall!* or *You'll never amount to much!* or *Who do you think you are?* or *Don't think you can change the world!* or… well, fill in the blank with the ones you might have heard. This often leaves us with a thick residue of hopelessness or helplessness. The point here is to question our limits, to not automatically settle within them. In addition to being kind to ourselves by not overworking or being anxious, we can ask ourselves questions like: *Why not? What would it take to accomplish a bigger vision for my YouthBuild? What capacity would be needed? Whom could I enlist to help? How do I overcome my internal obstacles? What is my own vision? How do I keep my eyes on the prize?* And so on.

The elements are interdependent. A moment's thought about various vision elements outlined above will make clear that they are highly interactive, overlapping, and mutually reinforcing elements. For example, the deeper the personal counseling is, the more the young people mature emotionally. The more they mature emotionally, the more seriously they take their education. The more relevant the YouthBuild education to them, the more they tend to learn and succeed in furthering their education. The more that leadership is emphasized, the more the students' identities and aspirations change in an upward direction. The more the culture of YouthBuild is welcoming, positive, and inclusive, the more ownership young people take for the program, the better the program goes, the more they show up, and so the program outcomes tend to be higher, thus positioning the program for sustainability. And so on.

Highlighting parts of the vision. Though each of these vision elements is important, for the remainder of this book I am going to focus on only a handful of the elements, the ones that I know most about and I think are central: program values and culture, staff building, leadership development, education, counseling and healing, and graduate work.

4

Core Values
and Program Culture

THE HOPE AND THE CHALLENGE

*T*he photo below is of a group of YouthBuild directors. It represents YouthBuild staff. Can you see how happy, idealistic, and diverse they are, eager and ready to make a difference with the young people?

The next photo is what they meet on day one at YouthBuild!

You have seen this before—young people looking bored, thick with attitude, shut down, depressed, not expecting much, thinking things like *I've been through these kinds of programs before. I'll get a little money and maybe my GED, but I don't think this is for real.* Many young people raised in low-income neighborhoods with few resources who have been systematically disrespected or mistreated come to look and feel like this.

And the following photo, of a recent YouthBuild National Alumni Council, represents what we want! You can see the transformation fulfilled in this photo: young people who are confident, happy, close with each other, professional, have the look of being about business, clearly leaders. The challenge is to create conditions that help the young people who look like the ones above transform their lives so they look like the ones below.

What all YouthBuild directors and staff try their best to do is provide those conditions for young people to make this transformation. Besides a clear vision like the one sketched in the last chapter a transformational YouthBuild program rests on what might be called "the tripod of success," namely core values, program design and culture, and a strong, cohesive staff. What is the essence of what your program stands for; how does the culture and structure of the program reflect those values; and how do you build a staff unified around the core values and consistently implementing the program culture and design? We will examine the first two legs of the tripod in this chapter and the third, staff building, in the following chapter.

IMPORTANCE OF PROGRAM CORE VALUES

When I am facilitating a workshop on core values with a YouthBuild staff team, I usually begin by asking each staff person to write down on a three-by-five index card one or two words that best express what they think the program stands for. We post the cards on the wall and then take a look. Five individuals on a staff might come up with a list like this:

- Discipline

- Job preparation

- Leadership

- Love

- Empowerment

This is a fine set of values, and it is quite typical. If you were the director, you might feel happy to get this list. However, there are some fault lines in such a list that point to the importance of having a unified and tight set of core values.

Perhaps the construction manager, whose training was in the Marines, believes that discipline is the key to success and when young people mess up they should be held accountable, disciplined, and told to suck up their feelings. Besides, there is a building to finish, on time and on budget. But the counselor, whose training was in social work school and clinical experience, believes that young people need love and acceptance first, no matter their behavior, and be given second and third and fourth chances until they grow into more positive behavior. Expressing their feelings in a counseling session will help change negative behavior, says the counselor. The construction staff thinks the counselor just sits all day in an air-conditioned office and does little except talk about feelings with the young people and doesn't prepare them for the real world. The counselor thinks the construction manager is too hard and strict, and that he doesn't understand the trauma that makes the young people act out the way they do. She thinks building the person is ultimately more important than building the building.

Or maybe the teacher and director are about developing the leadership skills and confidence of the students and encouraging them to make decisions and feel that they can make a difference. But the job developer knows that the employers he is trying to line up as job placements don't want "empowered leaders" at the entry level; they want somebody who shows up, does a good day's work, and doesn't cause trouble. He thinks this empowerment stuff misleads the young people about the world of work.

Granted, these are straw figures, but these kinds of tensions are quite typical on a YouthBuild staff that has not done work on agreeing to a common set of program values. Of course, each of us comes to our work with our own individual set of values. This is as it should be. However, it is essential that each staff member understands, agrees with, and supports a set of common program values. Here are a few examples of sets of core values and beliefs.

The YouthBuild Philadelphia Charter School has three core values: respect, excellence, and perseverance. These three were arrived at through many staff conversations, unpacking the different meanings of these words, and asking how each would play out in the program. Now, all staff adhere to these core values. All programming is reviewed as to how it will advance these three values. Budgeting, fundraising, graduation standards, new initiatives, discipline policies, staff evaluations, leadership opportunities, service learning—everything is looked at through the lens of these three values.

Most YouthBuild programs have created a pledge that is recited on a regular daily basis by youth and staff. These pledges help the community internalize the core values. Here is the program pledge of the first YouthBuild program, Youth Action Program and Homes, in East Harlem, New York.

Youth Action YouthBuild Program Pledge

We, the members of the Youth Action YouthBuild Program, pledge that we are working together:

- To improve and rebuild our community
- To relate to each other in cooperative ways
- To develop our potential as leaders
- To educate and improve ourselves and help others along the way
- To respect our peers, neighbors, and all life, and
- To be part of a great movement for justice, equality and peace

All this we do with love and dignity.

Some YouthBuild programs have incorporated the core values from an educational methodology called Quantum Learning©.

Core Values of Quantum Learning

- Everything speaks
- Everything is on purpose
- Failure leads to success
- Strive for balance
- Live with integrity
- Live above the line (of responsibility)

YOUTHBUILD USA'S CORE
UNDERLYING CONVICTIONS & VALUES

YouthBuild USA's work is guided by the following core ideas, as stated on our website and in foundational documents, and elaborated here. For those readers who have been in YouthBuild for some time, these will be very familiar. But for newer YouthBuild staff these may need stating.

Sacred Life. Every human life is sacred, full of potential, and worthy of love.

Potential for a Just Society. Human beings have the potential to create a good society in which mutual respect and a reasonably just distribution of resources and opportunities are the dominant realities. Achieving such a society is the central challenge that faces us as a species.

Healthy Communities. Individuals are decisively influenced by the communities in which they are raised and in which they live. Communities that have a rich set of opportunities, caring relationships, high expectations, positive values, and that are organized to meet the needs of their members and the children within them, are the foundation of a healthy society.

Leadership. Every community and society needs ethical, caring, committed leaders who have the best interests of the community members at heart and are skilled in bringing people together to set goals, implement ideas, and solve problems. Leadership development is at the heart of community development. Young people are capable of playing a leadership role and if encouraged to do so will bring enormous energy, creativity, and imagination to the work.

Love. When young people feel loved and cared for, their respect for themselves and other people grows. They are more likely to realize their true potential and to accomplish their highest goals. They grow eager to give back, and to have a positive influence on the lives of others. YouthBuild immerses young men and women in a nurturing environment that provides structure and direction as well as care and appreciation. They know that the staff's commitment to helping them overcome personal obstacles and negative patterns is deeply rooted in respect for the intelligence and potential of each trainee. In each YouthBuild mini-community, young people make new friends committed to a positive lifestyle.

Knowledge. Young people growing up in poor neighborhoods desire skills to help them move forward in life. However, they are often discouraged by an education system that fails to recognize their intelligence, fails to help them overcome learning difficulties, and fails to make learning a meaningful and exciting part of their lives. YouthBuild offers a dynamic alternative. Its personalized, self-paced educational program is a powerful blend of experiential and academic learning that frees students' innate intellectual and creative ability. They soon learn to see math and reading as practical skills needed to accomplish tasks in their daily lives. Teachers work closely with each student to ensure that no one is overlooked. At the same time, YouthBuild's philosophy of peer-assisted learning builds trust and confidence among trainees.

Responsibility. Growing up in poverty subverts the hopes and dreams of too many young people before they ever get started. A dramatic change is essential for these young men and women to move forward and take responsibility for their lives. YouthBuild offers a safe and supportive environment where life-altering shifts can occur. It inspires young people to meet new challenges at the work site and in the classroom, and trainees learn to be accountable as individuals and as members of a team. At each YouthBuild, young people actively participate in the governance of their program through an elected policy committee. By graduation, trainees have learned to take responsibility for themselves, for their families, and for their communities.

Respect. Respect is a two-way street. People who feel respected and appreciated are more likely to respect and appreciate others. When young people who have been stigmatized and discredited are respected, they find the freedom to give up their old negative, self-defeating attitudes. Opportunities to earn respect abound at YouthBuild. Whether renovating an abandoned building, speaking at a public hearing, or helping a classmate master geometry, trainees soon demonstrate hidden skills and talents. In meeting these challenges, they earn the respect of their co-workers and supervisors. By taking part in the rebuilding of their neighborhoods, trainees gain the respect of their communities and act as visible role models. The more they are recognized for their accomplishments, the more they value themselves and other people.

PROGRAM CULTURE: EVERYTHING SPEAKS!

Core values can be some words on a page that get pulled out only when writing a funding proposal, or they can be a living code that is internalized and operationalized by the program. This latter situation is best accomplished through the program culture, that is, the program's look and feel plus its language, rituals, standards, celebrations, approaches to discipline, relationships among students and staff, and so on.

To borrow a phrase from Quantum Learning®, "Everything speaks." Everything communicates something. What "speaks" in a program? The colors on the walls speak. The posters on the wall speak. The arrangement of the furniture in the classroom speaks. The diversity of the staff speaks. The staff tone of voice speaks. Who speaks most speaks. Who has what kind of power speaks. What is taught and what is being learned speaks. What outcomes the program achieves speaks. What gains young people make speaks. And so on about every aspect of a program.

Each program has a culture, whether intentional or not. The question is, to what extent is the culture speaking the core values and vision? In my experience, a program that has not done enough work on honing a commonly shared set of core values usually has a sloppy and incoherent program culture. Why? Because in the absence of commonly held *program* values, individuals rely on their *personal* set of values, and that can lead to tensions like the ones described earlier.

Step one is to engage the program staff (and perhaps the sponsoring agency) in definitive dialogue about what the program most stands for and the core values that guide the program. Most YouthBuild programs have adopted some version of YouthBuild core values stated above. In well-functioning YouthBuild programs, the staff who are hired must share those core values. As mentioned earlier, when working with a program that has not established its core values, I often begin by asking each staff person to post the one or two words that he or she thinks best represents what the program stands for. Then each person talks about why each value is important. Each person's starting point is validated and respected. If there are differences in emphasis, as in the illustrative list of five above, then the group unpacks how there might be tensions among these, especially around behavior and discipline. The staff continues talking and listening, maybe over several weeks, until each staff person can come to understand and agree to live by a short set of common program values when they are acting as YouthBuild staff. A skilled facilitator can help land this discussion in a solid place. The facilitator could present various program scenarios for staff to roleplay to clarify how to handle the scene that would be most consistent with the program values. Maybe each staff member presents his or her understanding of the program values.

The next step is to thoroughly assess the current program culture to see which parts align with the set of core values and which need to be brought into alignment. This needs to be a clear-eyed look at the way things operate and why each piece is in place. In an established program, there may be some sacred cows that might need to come under scrutiny and not be continued just because "we've always done it that way" if it no longer fits with the core values.

Once a coherent set of core program values is established, staff can take another look at the program design, the staffing pattern, the staff qualifications (more on this in the next chapter), the systems of supervision and accountability, the student handbook and guidelines, the youth recruitment and selection criteria, the look and feel of the physical space, the classroom curricula, the integration of all components, the rituals and processes through which values are taught, and so on.

If the program doesn't have a pledge that the students recite daily, start there!

A PICTURE OF PROGRAM CULTURE

From the photo below, what would you guess about this YouthBuild program's culture? What is speaking?

You would probably point out the following things: the program values cooperative learning; the students seem engaged and respectful of each other; there is a physical comfort and closeness; a sense of enjoying each other; leadership and productivity seem present; students have access to computers for learning; students' art work or drawings are posted on wall above computers; the timeline they are constructing is about Asian Americans (thus they are studying a group different from themselves); diversity is valued. Even this one snapshot reveals a lot about a program.

YOUTHBUILD USA's RESEARCH ON PROGRAM CULTURE

In 2005, senior staff at YouthBuild USA conducted interviews with the directors and staff of the 20 programs with the then-highest performance outcomes to determine how those programs achieved their high outcomes. Among the findings one thing stood out: all the programs had a coherent, consistent, and clear culture that permeated the program. All staff were trained in the approach and were expected to implement it.

One program used a thinking-process program called TruThought as its base. TruThought, an approach that comes out of the substance-abuse field, works on making conscious the thought patterns that precede and accompany any action. For example, if Kevin stole money from the "swear jar," the staff would ask him what he was thinking as he did this, to help Kevin understand that he could think and act differently next time. All program staff are sent to a TruThought training shortly after they are hired.

Another program used an asset-based, community leadership approach, grounded in an analysis of oppression. The program hired staff from the community who had backgrounds similar to those of the students, expected students to be leaders, and challenged students to question the conditions that damaged their communities and families.

Another program incorporated Quantum Learning as its program methodology, not just its classroom approach. Quantum Learning's "eight keys of excellence" are painted on the walls. All staff get trained in using Quantum Learning; the programs expects students to "live above the line of responsibility."

Yet another program used restorative practices as the method for handling discipline and resolving conflict. Rather than a punishment model, restorative practices is based on a model of restoring ruptured relationships or making restitution of damages. It asks the parties involved questions like *What did you learn? What do you need to do to fix it?*

One program instituted a thoroughgoing practice of shout-outs. In classrooms, on the worksite, and in community meetings, private and public appreciations are given out freely and often. Each Friday's assembly is a love-fest of appreciative shout-outs for students, for staff, for administrative folks, for visitors. First modeled by staff, as time goes on every student has tasted the good vibes of this practice and begins to spontaneously pass it on. See chapter 8 for examples of using appreciations and shout-outs.

You can see from these few examples that, within limits, the exact methodology or approach applied to a program culture can vary. And though there was a wide range of approaches, at the base none of them contradict YouthBuild's core values. The data from these interviews points to the correlation between high program outcomes (a practical consideration for funding) and core values and culture.

The chart below summarizes some key culture-building elements of an effective YouthBuild program.

Program-wide Elements That Support Positive Outcomes and Personal Transformation

- Program philosophy or method, clear core values
- A thorough youth orientation
- A coherent program design and solid program components
- A contract and infraction system, consistent discipline
- A pledge recited by the group that internalizes values
- Rituals, recognitions, and/or rites of passage
- Social, cultural, and community-building activities
- Youth participation in decision making
- Thoroughgoing mutual respect
- Leadership development opportunities

INTEGRATION OF PROGRAM COMPONENTS

Another piece of a building a coherent program is the successful integration of all its components.

When I have had the opportunity to work with new sites in their early development, I often ask the director and staff to consider the program they had designed or described in their funding proposal. I then ask them to imagine that they were young people going through that program and ask themselves: *Would I, as a young person, feel that there is a consistent group of skilled adults who are caring about my development and who are in sync with each other, or would I feel farmed out to this GED outfit over here, and that housing developer over there, and this counseling service over here, and that job placement center over there, and that each staff person was using a different way of dealing with me? Or would I feel there is a central "home" that I could count on that is safe from emotional and physical harm, and where I am known, accepted, and cared for by a kind and skilled group of adults who are pointing all us young people in a good direction?*

Or not? If not, then the program design, core values, and program culture are in need of alignment.

The point of all the collective work in YouthBuild—of all the money, of all the time, of all the heartache—is that young person after young person should have the chance to transform their lives for the better and reach for the highest human potential. The young people, whether they can articulate this or not, are looking for the right conditions to make those big changes. So if we begin with this end in mind, how might the five program components be thoroughly integrated?

The Five Program Components of YouthBuild

Construction +
Supervised training • Building homes • Employer expectations • Job readiness skills • Vocational education • Pre-apprenticeship • Industry-recognized certifications • Other vocational training

Education
Academic skills • GED, GED Plus, and HS diploma preparation • Vocational skills • Job & college readiness • Construction terms • Cultural education

Leadership
Decision making • Group facilitation • Leadership roles • Leadership competencies • Public speaking • Negotiating • Community service • Advocacy

Counseling
Peer, individual, and group counseling • Case-management outside referrals • Life skills • Life goals

Graduate resources
College & career counseling • Pre-employment and pre-apprenticeship training • Placement monitoring • Alumni clubs • Mentoring • Leadership

We might ask ourselves questions like:

- How does the program need to be designed and delivered to maximize transformation?

- How do we create a caring home base for the young people?

- What would the program culture look like? What core values would it "speak"?

- How would the classroom, construction, counseling, and leadership-development components work together to promote transformation?

- How would we start planning for "after graduation" at the beginning of the program?

- How would we orient our students to the world of work and higher education from day one?

- How would leadership development be integrated throughout the program so it's not just a workshop on Friday afternoons?

- In how many ways could we engage young people in decision making?

- How could construction or other training-track staff be trained in teaching and counseling skills?

- How could the program be structured and staffed to provide the deep safety needed by young people to help heal old hurts and trauma?

- How could the teacher have students write about the construction process or tool safety and how could the construction trainer incorporate math for the GED on the worksite?

- How would life skills be woven across components?

- How would we build in formal mentoring relationships?

- What structures would allow a construction trainer, a teacher, and a counselor to think regularly about a specific group of young people in the program?

- While doing green building, how can the construction staff and teachers raise students' awareness about why we do green building and how it impacts climate change issues?

- How do we build a positive peer culture that supports young people?

- How do we engage the students in wider community service so that they come to care even more about their neighborhoods and know that they can make a difference?

These and other questions help us figure out how to increasingly integrate all parts of the YouthBuild program into a cohesive whole. We will unpack some of these questions in future chapters. In my observation over the years, among the most successful YouthBuild programs are those that were either created to do YouthBuild solely or have the full support of the sponsoring organization, and where the YouthBuild program has control over program design, hires its own staff, coordinates all the components under one roof, and is able to create a unified staff that supports a commonly held set of values and a consistent program culture.

YOUTHBUILD QUALITIES AND CULTURE FOR TRANSFORMATION

On the one side there is the program design, a comprehensive blend of construction training or other career training, educational improvement, personal counseling, leadership development, and graduate resources upon completion of the program. Program design elements are clearly and usefully laid out in the *YouthBuild Program Design and Performance Standards* document developed through democratic processes every five years. On the other side, equally valuable and just as fundamental, is the assessment of qualities inherent to the components of a meaningful and integrated program.

In YouthBuild, one way of determining what these qualities need to be is to analyze the consistent mistreatment the young people in our programs have experienced, and chart a course directly opposite to these past experiences. As Dorothy Stoneman has said,

> Our young people have lived in relative poverty and powerlessness in an affluent society that has given them little respect and few opportunities, and has not cared enough about them to protect them from the temptations of drugs, the physical decay of their environment, the breakdown of their families and overwork of their parents, and even homelessness and hunger. Many of them have also experienced

racism or discrimination against immigrants. To succeed to the maximum extent, a program must dramatically reverse this past experience. It should correct the shortcomings of the institutions and attitudes that have so far disappointed and hurt our young people.

A YouthBuild program must, therefore, include the following elements and qualities of positive culture. (Some of the following items might be considered core values. The bolded subheadings constitute a list originally put forth by Dorothy Stoneman, which is included in the *YouthBuild Affiliated Network Design and Performance Standards*. I wrote the narrative to expand on each one.)

1. **Profound respect for the intelligence of young people**. Most young people who are poor have had their intelligence graded, judged, and maligned as inadequate. Furthermore, the adult world rarely takes the ideas of young people seriously. And yet, young people have innate intelligence waiting to be put to good use. The cornerstone of a transformational program is making respect for this intelligence real. How? Mainly by asking questions, listening deeply, implementing the ideas of young people. John Rivera, as a participant in the Youth Action Program, the first YouthBuild, was once asked to state the essence of the program. He replied, "It is the question: What do *you* think?"

2. **Young people's power over their immediate environment.** In addition to having their ideas dismissed and ignored, young people are excluded from decision-making power over the things that affect their lives—things like the conditions of the neighborhood, the quality of the schools, family finances, police practices, the location of recreation facilities, and so on. Therefore, a key practice of a solid youth-development program is to find as many ways as possible to include young people in decision making. This can run the gamut from simply asking young people what they think about things to expecting leadership, to formal consultation, to official policy power. In a YouthBuild program, the policy

committee, composed of elected young people, a staff representative, and the director, is expected to get serious training and have major decision-making responsibility for hiring staff, reviewing the agency budget, developing and enhancing program policies and initiatives, and setting direction for the program.

3. **Protection from disaster, or at least the support necessary to survive it.** A program must be safe. This is the major concern of young people at the outset. Is it physically and emotionally safe here? How much can I trust these people? These are the appropriate questions given the hard-learned lessons of survival in the often harsh environments of their lives. Practically, protection means establishing a group norm of respect, support, appreciation, acceptance, with no put-downs, and eventually a caring community. It also means being there at family funerals, hospital beds, court hearings, and job interviews.

4. **Meaningful work.** A transformational youth program is not doing just workforce development, which is often organized from the employer's point of view, but is providing the skills and motivation to create a meaningful work life. One of the reasons YouthBuild has focused on building affordable housing is that it is a tangible contribution to the community in which the program participants live. The young people walk home with pride as they wear their tool belts and hard hats. They show pride in their work as they give visitors a tour of the house. They feel pride when they see a formerly homeless family move into the house they just built. The point is that a solid youth-development program needs to choose a career-training track that has meaning, substance, and service at its heart.

5. **Patient caring for their development.** In addition to strengths and talents, young people come with a mix of bad habits, poor attitudes, low self-estimation, lack of trust, and experiences of frustration or failure in school. A solid YouthBuild program has

skilled staff and a consistent methodology that helps young people work through their obstacles on the way to achieving success.

6. **Teaching of skills.** The young people consistently report that they want caring staff, but they also want staff who know something and can teach them new skills. This is a necessary element of changing their lives—learning effective skills and tools. So ideally YouthBuild programs would be staffed by experts in their fields, who act with and model professional ways of communicating, networking, and planning, and who are able to share with students their own pathways to success and tips on how to achieve it.

7. **Firm and loving challenge to stop self-destructive behavior and negative attitudes.** Most YouthBuild students are survivors who live by acquiring street smarts—learning from peers rather than printed material or academic learning. Many perceive that society's structure is not for them, that society has no room for them. They live by their wits, sometimes outside the law, outside the cultural mainstream; sometimes violence, crime, and drug use may be significant factors in their lives, and renouncing this lifestyle to join an alternative training and academic program may be extremely difficult. In addition, they may have been out of school for a long time and think that they have failed repeatedly. Such young people usually join YouthBuild with a mixture of courage and desperation. They are enraged, afraid, and disenchanted. Therefore, working as a staff in a YouthBuild program is not for the faint of heart. The program needs to have a culture, a consistent approach, and a staff skilled enough to help young people change. Staff need to set clear policies for behavior, to be able to interrupt acting out with firmness and love. They need to be able to teach what behaviors are self-destructive and help students substitute new behaviors that build positive habits and reputation. Some staff need to be trained and willing to wade into the deeper developmental or trauma areas of young people's lives to help facilitate healing and more intelligent choices.

8. **Consistently positive values.** The program and staff need to create a culture where young people come to see that it is desirable to learn, to stop doing drugs, to adopt a positive lifestyle, to hang with positive people, to value honesty and integrity, to care about others and the world. Since the young people's distrust and cynicism are deep, the staff must be trustworthy and positive beyond reproach. The students are always watching the staff, so signs of corruption, selfishness, meanness, carelessness, or other negative characteristics expressed by the staff will undermine the power of the program and must be weeded out by management. The program pledge, community service, and leadership development all help to reinforce positive values.

9. **Family-like support and appreciation from peers and adults.** The program needs to become a healthy alternative community full of caring, appreciation, good feelings, acceptance, and safety to grow. It is essential to build a community to provide the support and strength to stick with the program, endure the pressures of new learning, accept the challenge to change old habits, to become literate, to opt out of the street culture, to set goals and reach for higher aspirations. When a YouthBuild program is succeeding, the students will say something like this: *I came here looking for a job and a GED, and what I found was a family. They cared about me more than I ever experienced or expected. As a result, now I care about myself and other people.*

10. **High standards and expectations.** Since most YouthBuild young people have been subject to society's dismissal and low expectations of them, the program needs to counteract that by setting realistic but high expectations for their achievement, performance, behavior, social relationships. High expectations need to be balanced with patient support to overcome self-doubt or anticipation of failure. All this is difficult to establish but absolutely necessary.

11. **Inspiring and caring role models who have overcome similar obstacles.** Young people need to see people like themselves who have succeeded despite hardships as living examples that it is possible to change one's life. The YouthBuild staff must include people in highly responsible roles from the students' racial or cultural backgrounds and people who have had some similar obstacles. YouthBuild graduates who are hired as staff because of their skills and qualities can provide the role models closest to students: *If he can do it, so can I.*

12. **Understanding of the proud and unique history of their people.** Peoples of all shades, backgrounds, and class origins have contributed mightily to this country and the world. However, racism, poverty, and the dominant culture have ignored, distorted, or undervalued this history. One YouthBuild program value is to help the young people develop awareness of and pride in their backgrounds.

13. **Heightened awareness of the present-day world and their important place in it.** A solid YouthBuild program gives real attention to helping young people understand current events and trends; the local, national, and global forces that are impacting their lives; and how they can negotiate their way through trying times as well as influence the policy makers whose decisions affect their communities.

14. **A path to future opportunities.** Young people will stay in Youth-Build if they can clearly see a payoff in terms of future jobs and continuing education. The program must be able to deliver. This means having a strong postsecondary education component, productive relationships with local employers, an effective graduate-resources program with mentors and support towards sustainable adult lives, and examples of young people who are successfully taking public leadership.

15. **A culture of rituals and practices shared in common by young people and staff.** The culture of the program is a pivotal element. The culture is formed by the beliefs, values, tone, rituals, and procedures that come to be shared by everyone, from young people to director. The culture needs to be consistent and intentional. Everything needs to reinforce everything. The culture consists of most of the items in this section, like shout-outs, appreciations, pledges, rites of passage, chants, graduations, consequences for violating basic values, and accountability of staff to perform consistently with those values.

16. **Concern and action from the sponsoring agency about changing the conditions that have affected the students and the people they love.** Young people want to be part of a greater effort to transform their communities. They respond positively to being part of an organization that is involved in making conditions better, in taking a stand against injustice, in being an advocate for communities.

17. **Fun.** Both formally and informally, the program encourages healthy laughter, positive ways of enjoying being together, and lots of raucous fun! This can take the form of games, barbecues, movie nights, camping trips, dances, silly times, talent shows, surprise outings, and more.

When the program design and culture are strong, young people tend to make great strides in their personal development and skill building. When these qualities and cultural styles are implemented well, young people immediately experience such respect and welcome that their orientation changes dramatically.

5

Building a Strong and Cohesive Staff

"Your job as staff in YouthBuild is not to focus on outcomes and deliverables, but to help young people understand their purpose in life. If you do that, high outcomes will follow."

Julian Ramirez, YouthBuild graduate and former staff, former president of the National Alumni Council, in his keynote address to National Directors Association, 2012

*I*n the last chapter, we looked at the first two legs of the tripod of success for a transformational YouthBuild program—core values and vision that point in the desired direction, and a program culture that speaks the core values in a thoroughgoing way. Now we turn to the third leg—building a strong and cohesive staff that supports the values, vision, and culture.

Staff building is an enormous topic. Books on staff hiring, training, supervision, accountability, development, promotion, discipline, teamwork, and similar topics fill shelves in libraries. My purpose here is not to review this literature but to offer a few reflections that are implied by YouthBuild's vision.

Throughout this book, I am trying to envision YouthBuild at its fullest potential, using its North Star as a guide. If I am a YouthBuild director and I want YouthBuild to be a powerful leadership training program; to promote college preparation and lifelong learning; to be an effective healing environment for the deep wounds of life; to promote real youth transformation; to be on the cutting edge of green building, green jobs, and green leadership; and to be a force for social change in the community, then I obviously can't do this alone, even if I do have a wonderful set of core values and an inspiring vision. So obviously the next critical piece is building a staff that can help carry this out.

ATTRIBUTES AND QUALITIES OF STAFF

Some of the key attributes and qualities that I would be looking for in staff are love; emotional health and maturity; competency, skill, and cooperation; leadership; integrity; diversity; and the embodiment of YouthBuild's core values.

Love

Love has been mentioned often so far as part of YouthBuild's core values and qualities. Initially, love mostly comes from the staff. So, first, I want staff who really like young people and have the ability to show their caring and love. Young people enter YouthBuild pretty beat up by poverty, racism, or abuse of all kinds. They may have been dodging bullets and the police. They may have been victims of sexual or domestic abuse. They may have been incarcerated. What do they need to find in YouthBuild? A sanctuary of safety and caring. They don't believe it at first. *No one ever cared about me before.* They push back and resist, testing to see if the staff are true, or, in their words, are "for real." For some young people, it is the first time they genuinely feel loved. They say things like:

They respected me. They didn't hold my past against me.

They came to my house to get me out of bed when I didn't show up for the program.

When my mother was in a coma, they came to the hospital.

When I got busted over the weekend for stupid stuff, they came and bailed me out and talked to the judge. No one ever did that for me.

Once basic trust is established, a young person is more willing to be open to what the program has to offer. As one YouthBuild counselor said, "They don't care what you know until they know that you care." Then they can take advantage of the learning opportunities, skill development, and leadership roles. As they grow in confidence and competence, they begin to show initiative and raise their aspirations. *Maybe I could go to college. Maybe I can start my own business. Maybe I can get out of my bad relationship. Maybe I* can *be somebody.* This message that first had to come from the outside—a caring staff and the program as a whole—now starts to be taken inside. As the process of transformation unfolds, a young person gradually makes a shift in identity.

YouthBuild young people are like the flowers that close up at night, only to open only to the warming rays of the sun each day. But if the staff keep beaming love, care, and respect at them, gradually, gradually, over time, in fits and starts, they open up. Along the way they may test and question and doubt and resist and give you the finger. But if the love and respect keep coming, slowly they will begin to trust. It is their nature to move towards their health and well-being.

So staff who work in my YouthBuild program would have to know that showing love is their first job. And it means sometimes going beyond the program hours, beyond the job description, beyond the boundaries that some people have been taught to maintain so they don't get too involved. It means showing up for young people at unexpected times. It means counteracting their assumptions that nobody cares. It means building deep relationships that matter.

So it is essential that each staff be able to show that love. It doesn't mean that all the love has to look the same. An ex-marine can show the kind of tough love that some young people really need at a certain stage of their development, maybe the caring father figure who believes in the student's potential and won't let him give in to his old habits of laziness or powerlessness. Other young people need the momma figure who says *Come here, sweetheart, you need a hug.* In many forms, the power of love is the foundation for transformation. (Obviously, all this assumes the appropriate awareness that nothing that smacks of flirtation or sexual harassment can be part of that expression of caring.)

Emotional health and maturity

In order to show love and caring to this extent, a staff member needs to have done his or her own personal work enough to be free of the fear of caring and commitment. Staff need to be comfortable with their own strong emotions and have healed much of their own traumas so that they can welcome the hurt of the young people without freaking out or getting knocked off their own emotional balance. I'm not saying that every YouthBuild staff person must be an enlightened being and have no issues, but each staff member should be emotionally healthy, have a strong positive identity, be able to listen well and not get reactive, be capable of making deep relationships that are not expressions of their own need, handle inevitable conflicts in a healthy way, and be able to hold out to young people a positive, hopeful vision of the future.

Competency, skill, and cooperation

Love is not enough on its own. Of course, each staff person needs to be very good at his or her job. Young people consistently say something like *They cared about me and they also had something to teach me.* As we all would ideally, I would hire a superb teacher, a superb construction staff, a superb counselor, and so on, all masters of their trades as well as superb teachers of their trades. And, because of the need to have a holistic, integrated program, each staff person needs to also be able to cross-train, to be a team player, to incorporate elements of other components into his or her area, and implement the program values, vision, and culture. All staff persons need to be so dedicated to the overall long-term mission and values that they are willing to take on almost any task for the team to further those goals, including those outside the job descriptions. They would all be able to form close, healthy, enjoyable relationships with other staff. They need to come through for young people, fulfill their promises, and model responsibility, consistency, competence, follow-through, and integrity.

Leadership

As will be clear in the next chapter, on the centrality of leadership development, I would hire staff who were leaders in their own right. For example, a construction manager who was active in the local carpenters union, a teacher who was part of a progressive teacher community, a counselor/case manager who was active in local community affairs, a career counselor who belonged to the Rotary Club, a leadership developer who had worked in political campaigns, and so on. I would be clear with staff that their second job, after respecting and caring about the young people, was to develop the students' leadership potential. I would want staff to take young people with them to meetings of their trade unions, business associations, and social justice groups. I would expect staff to expose young people to the larger community and wider issues than they might have had contact with so far, and introduce them to community leaders. I would expect staff to be concerned about world affairs and actively bring current events into their discussions with young people, as part of raising their awareness about the world. I would hire staff who had a humanistic and positive vision for society, their own version of Dr. King's "beloved community."

I would hire staff who will ask young people to see more clearly and not accept the negative messages that they got hammered with. Tyra Johnson, a student from Los Angeles, said, "YouthBuild is like a windshield wiper. My life is the windshield. It has been rained on and hit with rocks many times throughout my life. The windshield wiper of YouthBuild swept away everything so that my vision became clear. For the first time in a long time, I am able to see where I am heading."

Integrity

Most YouthBuild young people have seen corruption at all levels of society, from the highest levels of power to the street level: lying, stealing, cheating, getting over, fronting, threatening, gossiping, slandering, bad-rapping, manipulating, dominating and surrendering. To develop trust and gain confidence, young people need to be with staff who have personal integrity; who do what they say they will do; who walk their talk; who live the core values; who never lie or cheat; who are not greedy or selfish, mean or cruel, careless or disrespectful; who can be emulated. The young people will test to see if staff are for real, sometimes repeatedly. They have been let down too many times to be easily snookered. But they want us to be straight. They need us to be for real. Sometimes this might require staff to be open and honest about how decisions are made in the program, or even how they handle some of their own personal challenges (within appropriate boundaries). Transparency is key for building trust.

Diversity

Increasingly, young people will live and work in a diverse world, with people very different from themselves. Part of their positive development is to learn what is sometimes called "cultural competence." To me this means, on the one hand, to embrace their own identities around race, culture, gender, sexual orientation, and so on, and then to clean up the self-limiting or unhealthy parts of those identities. On the other hand, it means to respect and learn from others unlike themselves.

Therefore, I would hire a diverse staff with cultural competence. Young people need to see some staff members who look like them and come from similar backgrounds so they can see that others like them have made it, and be able to think *So I can do it, too.* They also need staff from different backgrounds but who have a lot to offer in terms of different perspectives, contacts, experiences, and ideas of what is possible. Being respected and valued by people from different backgrounds, including the dominant culture, counteracts the internalized feelings of being devalued by people in authority. Our experience in YouthBuild is that solid, helpful, deep relationships happen across all differences—that from a young person's point of view, what matters is that the adult is a genuine, caring human being, and accepts the young person for whom he or she is.

In addition, since a YouthBuild program mirrors the wider society in that the issues of oppression and diversity are present, I would hire staff who had done a lot of work on their own diversity issues and were able to engage with other staff in frank and respectful discussions of the issues, work them through, and continue to be in good relationship with each other. I would make clear that YouthBuild considers its diversity in staffing as an organizational asset and that we will be actively exploring these assets as a program, with each other and with the students. (For more on this topic, see my handbook *Creating a Diverse Community at YouthBuild.*)

Embodiment of core values
Since core values are central for me, I would select staff who as much as possible have already embodied those program values and have already implemented them in their other work situations.

HIRING PROCESS TIPS

Most of the attributes and capacities above are not the ones that are typically listed in a job posting or set of qualifications, but these are the ones I would be looking for, as would any YouthBuild director with an integrated vision for YouthBuild. How to get these staff members is a different question. Sometimes YouthBuild directors are unable to hire their own staff due to policies of the sponsoring organization, the constraints of the education partnerships, and so on. These can be challenging obstacles that requires creative maneuvering to get around. Again, there are many good books on staff hiring, and there is helpful information in the *YouthBuild Program Handbook.* Here are a few key points from my experience.

Make it hard to get hired.
It would be extremely hard to be hired at my YouthBuild program. The candidate would be put through many hoops. When I was a young teacher, I applied to teach at a parent-run community storefront school in East Harlem in New York City. The interview process was an eye-opening and humbling experience. I was interviewed by the parents of children in this elementary school. All were low-income, half of them spoke English, and half of them spoke only Spanish. But they were in charge of their school and their children's education. They gave me the most grueling and thorough interview and hiring process I have ever had, before or since. They asked me about everything. They wanted to know who I was as a person, what I cared about, why I wanted to teach, what my values and character were. They wanted to sense how I would be with and for their children. The second interview was held in the storefront classroom. Some of their children were playing nearby and a second-grader had taken the snake out of the terrarium. Spontaneously, one of the parent interviewers asked me to get the child to put the snake back into the terrarium. They watched closely. They were watching for tone of voice, level of respect, skill of interaction, and effectiveness of my approach. Fortunately, I passed the test. It was a good example of having a high bar for hiring.

Robert Burkhardt, a friend of mine who was the founding director of Eagle Rock School, a high quality, value-based innovative residential high school for YouthBuild-type young people in the foothills of the

Colorado Rocky Mountains, described one his methods for interviewing prospective staff: Immediately upon arrival at the secluded school, at the 8000-foot elevation, where the air is thinner, he invites the job candidate to take a walk with him. They climb up a challenging rocky path to a gorgeous peak with a grand view of the Rockies. If the candidate huffs and curses and complains on the way up, he concludes that the interview is over. If the candidate puts attention primarily on the stunning beauty rather than on the hard climb, Burkhardt concludes that the candidate is worth a further look.

Have applicants demonstrate their skills and approaches.
The point of these two stories is to put a prospective candidate through some trials to test their mettle. For YouthBuild, I would have a teacher candidate teach a class; the construction staff would work for a day on the worksite alongside the young people; the counselor would be asked to run a group or do a life-skills workshop; a job developer might help a group of students create their résumés, and so on. This is common practice for excellent YouthBuild programs.

Hold a series of interviews that include young people.
If after a first interview with me a candidate met my basic requirements (openly caring, emotionally healthy, skilled in their field, was a leader, added a dimension of diversity, had integrity, and embodied most of the core values of the program), then a group of young people would interview the candidate. Preparation of the young people for the interview is critical. What qualities and skills are we looking for? How can we know if the candidate is qualified and fits with Youth-Build? What kinds of interview questions should we ask or not ask? Young people should also interview more than one candidate to surface points of comparison. With this preparation, young people can sniff out quickly who is for real, who shows them true respect, who listens well, who knows their stuff, who can relate. This is also good leadership training for the young people, and offers them more ownership of the program.

Hiring staff is a huge responsibility that counteracts some previous experiences of being excluded from meaningful decisions. The director would also be well-advised not to hire anyone that the young people reject. Likewise, if the young people are involved in the hiring decision, the director cannot abdicate his or her own good judgment if it differs from the young people. This needs to be a mutual decision. The director should refer to the young people for interviews only candidates that are acceptable. References should be checked prior to the young people's interviews, so that they can be reminded how critical references are.

I would also then involve other staff in interviewing each prospective candidate, depending on time, size of staff, and position being selected. This provides the candidate with a good view of the staff and their personalities, skills, and diversity. Often a candidate will ask other staff what it's like to work at YouthBuild. This allows staff to talk about the core values, vision, program culture, teamwork, integration across components, and diversity of the staff. A candidate can assess how they fit with these descriptions. Involving staff in the interview process provides more perspective and feedback on the candidate and allows them to be part of the process of adding someone to the team, since teamwork is essential element of a solid YouthBuild program. Staff ownership and accountability increase.

Do deep reference checks.
Reference checks are standard, of course, but there are couple of things I would be sure to do. I would invite a young person to listen in as part of the leadership-training component, and I'd dig for insight about the key attributes and qualifications we were looking for. In addition to the more routine questions about experience and skill, I would ask for examples of how the candidate showed caring and respect, handled a conflict situation, and exhibited emotional stability. I'd ask what leadership roles the candidate played in the organization and in the wider world, when he or she modeled integrity or showed cultural competence. I would ask, "If we hired this person a year from now, what

would I love about the person and his or her work and accomplishments, and what would annoy me or get under my skin?" My practice is to do this reference check with at least the candidate's last three supervisors, and anyone else they recommend.

Wait for the right one.
This is easier said than done, given availability of candidates, timing, program needs, and so on. But ideally, I would give myself enough lead time to search and recruit until the right candidate surfaced. I might have to let the position go unfilled for a while, or even hire a temporary staff member while I continue looking. I remember the director of one YouthBuild program who was determined to hire a woman construction trainer in order to attract more women into YouthBuild and ultimately into the trades. None were in sight at the time, so he hired a male construction staff on a temporary basis until a qualified female trainer was found.

Building a diverse staff is often a challenge. Over the years of hiring at YouthBuild USA, given societal demographics, I consistently receive many more résumés from qualified white candidates for each qualified candidate of color. Unless I am clear about building a racially and culturally diverse staff, all the positions could easily be filled by white folks. You need to build a diverse pool of qualified candidates before making a decision—doing this is a legally acceptable process, whereas choosing a candidate based on race or gender is not. Current program staff and the sponsoring organization need to understand the need for diversity. This is another reason for having clarity on values and vision. Sometimes you just have to wait until you have a diverse pool of qualified candidates.

CREATING STAFF COHESION

I hope it is clear by this point in the book that core values, program design and culture, and staff cohesion are mutually interdependent. Staff cohesion is not automatic, but it will be easier to create and maintain if the core values are clear, the mission is strong, and the staff are competent and aligned with the values and mission as closely as possible.

Program Success Trio

Core values

Staff cohesion

Program culture

The director is the leader of the staff. It is the director who sets the tone and shapes the contours of staff cohesion. Here are a few of my reflections, to augment the information on this topic that can be found in numerous good books and in the *YouthBuild Program Handbook.*

Modeling cohesion-building practices

The first is that the director, above all, needs to be a living example of the qualities sought in other staff. If I were the director, in order to build a strong, cohesive staff able to carry out a powerful transformational YouthBuild program, I would need to respect and care about the staff, demonstrate emotional health, walk my talk, live by my principles, support the program values, be a leader worth emulating, demonstrate commitment to diversity, and be very competent at directing the program. This is easier said than done, of course. This is why being a director is in itself a leadership-development path. Staff and young people alike are watching the director constantly for indications of integrity, emotional maturity, and sound policy.

Caring for staff

As director, I would care about my staff. I would get to know them personally and professionally and show interest in them. I would make a practice of publicly and privately appreciating them, applauding them for specific accomplishments, noticing and praising their good performance. I would caringly coach them on their shortfalls or areas needing improvement, either directly or through their immediate supervisor—done as an ally caring about their development, not as a critic out to get them. I would invest in their professional development, send them to trainings, provide in-house skill improvement. I would find ways to support a good work-life balance—making sure staff did not overwork, insisting that they take their vacations, providing an employee-assistance program, budgeting for staff retreats and adequate planning time, and so on. We need to care about ourselves and our staff as much as we care about the young people. Furthermore, if the staff feel respected and cared about, they are likely to have even more motivation to create that kind of program culture for the young people.

Instilling core values

As director, I would take the lead on instilling and internalizing core values and vision. We would read and discuss the values and vision; really dialogue about what each part means, how it would look, what it implies about our functioning as individuals and as a team. This would be an iterative process, over time, checking for understanding of and moving towards agreement with each part. Where there is disagreement, we would work it through to a satisfactory resolution. We would periodically hold up one of the values or one piece of the vision to assess how well we are aligned with it. We would find creative ways to keep the values and vision fresh.

Co-creating program culture

As director, I would orchestrate an ongoing process of engaging the staff and students in building the program culture that reflected and reinforced the values and vision. To reiterate some of the ideas from the last chapter, we would examine everything for what is speaking and what values are being promoted; recite a values-laden YouthBuild pledge daily; ask staff and students to illustrate core values through skits, artwork, behavior; solve conflicts through a lens of values and vision; institute and support centers of staff decision making as well as youth decision making; and create consistent rituals, language, celebrations, expectations, and norms that operationalize the values and vision.

One of the most useful and succinct discussions of building staff cohesion is Dorothy Stoneman's article "The Art and Challenge of Being a YouthBuild Director." In it she identifies ten not-so-unusal practices that, when taken together, contribute solidly to staff unity. The illustration below lists them. I recommend the complete article.

10 Key Ingredients for Staff Team Building

1. Regular meetings
2. Effective listening
3. Supervision and praise
4. Sharing of information
5. Sharing of decision making

6. No overwork
7. Staff training
8. Inviting and accepting criticism
9. Diversity issues
10. Firing

A CLOSING NOTE

Hiring the right staff and building a high-performing team are daunting tasks, but they are critically important. One successful YouthBuild director summarized her approach by saying she hires "high-functioning, low-maintenance" staff.

But some caveats are in order. I know I have presented an ideal scenario that rarely matches reality. In some towns and rural areas, the potential pool of candidates may be very small. Or, even when you think you have hired the right people, things go horribly wrong. Or, maybe you have the perfect team, then one person leaves and the replacement upsets the apple cart. Or, perhaps you inherited a staff that has not embraced the core values and North Star of YouthBuild, and need to be retrained. This is the real world, after all. Nonetheless, if you want a YouthBuild that reaches its full potential, there is no substitute for finding, creating, developing, caring about, and maintaining a strong, competent, and cohesive staff. This takes sustained intention and attention. Everything speaks!

6

Leadership Development

"The main thing is to keep the main thing the main thing."

Stephen Covey

YOUTHBUILD AS SOCIAL CHANGE, SOCIAL JUSTICE

By the end of this chapter it is my hope that you will be thoroughly persuaded that YouthBuild's main thing is the development of young leaders as a key component of following YouthBuild's North Star. I intend to make the case for this, sketch a vision of a robust leadership development approach, and focus on three key parts of leadership development: involving young people in decision-making through an effective program policy committee, integrating leadership development throughout the program, and using a set of leadership competencies as part of graduation requirements. For veterans of YouthBuild, especially those who have experienced any of my numerous leadership development workshops, this may be familiar territory. I hope this chapter motivates you to double down on your leadership development work. For those newer to YouthBuild, I hope it inspires you to think of leadership development as *your* main thing, no matter your job title.

Long-range goal

I have always viewed YouthBuild as a step toward the long-range goal of fundamental societal change. For me this will mean the end of all oppression; a just economic distribution of goods, services, opportunities, and ownership; the use of production for real human need, not human greed or unnecessary consumption; the practice of thorough-going democracy; the flourishing of human creativity; respect and celebration of cultural differences; the end of violence as a means of solving conflict, whether personal or international; respect for our mother earth; an attitude of lifelong learning; and societal encouragement to explore deeper realms of existence, from inner or spiritual dimensions to microbial or deep-space dimensions.

I suspect that you and I share much of this vision for a decent world. The world we hunger for is not reachable in my lifetime. However, what we do in the present will help shape what is possible in the future and influence its creation.

Religious teachings about people in poverty as a guide

Down through history, people in low-income communities have absorbed the worst of human mistreatment, disrespect, and disregard. Great religious teachers have pointed to this inherent injustice and have organized great movements to correct this. Jesus said that "the poor will inherit the earth," and "what you do to the least of these, you do unto me." Gandhi organized India to accept "untouchables" into the ranks of humankind. Martin Luther King Jr. moved through a brilliant campaign of expanding civil rights for African Americans in this country, to conceiving of a massive "poor people's campaign" for economic justice, just prior to his death. Liberation theology, which has engendered powerful social-change movements in Latin America, puts the emphasis on the central role of poor people in creating a just world. YouthBuild, though not religious, in its social justice mission is squarely in this tradition.

Centrality of leadership

From its beginnings, YouthBuild was intended to be a movement-building effort aimed at bringing about what Martin Luther King Jr. called the "beloved community"—where opportunity, fairness, mutual responsibility, and social harmony prevail. In this movement, young people raised poor are a huge potential force for liberation. That is why YouthBuild has focused on the need for leadership development. Certainly we must do a lot of social service along the way, since the participants have real needs for housing, health care, food, legal help, family planning, and personal counseling. In addition, YouthBuild asks young people to develop themselves and to think beyond themselves, to see themselves as actors creating change rather than as clients getting services or victims getting abused. The following chart outlines the two approaches.

Social Service v. Social Change

Social service

- Helps people with real needs (housing, job training, education, legal, health, etc.)
- Is absolutely necessary
- Views people as clients or recipients of services

Social change

- Challenges injustice and inhuman structures
- Transforms root causes of injustice
- Engages people as leaders and decision makers
- Involves organizing, visioning, coalition building, and action

---

YouthBuild bridges these two concepts by providing the opportunity for young people to transform their own lives by being actors and leaders, by serving the community through building affordable housing and other service projects, by advancing their education, and by creating a positive, healthy peer community. This approach moves the young people out of being just "clients" getting services and points them in the direction of being change agents, as they emerge from their own individual survival stance.

One element of this perspective that Dorothy Stoneman has always discussed is the relevance of the language we use. For example, she recommends never calling the young people "clients" and instead calling them "students" because being a student involves taking initiative to learn and because students are respected in our larger culture. She also advises against referring to what we offer as "services" because services are seen as being delivered to passive recipients. Calling them "opportunities" is more appropriate because an opportunity requires an active person to seize them. Likewise, calling our students "kids" implies condescension, and calling the counselor a "case manager" is no good because nobody really wants to be a case that someone else manages.

Modern social-change movements, in my reading of them, have been a partnership between a recognized core of leaders able to articulate a vision and a strategy, and the mass of secondary leaders able to carry out the vision and strategy. And the vast majority who marched, fought, organized, went on strike, boycotted, sacrificed, went to jail, and made a difference were young people. Without the active leadership and involvement of young people, big change is not possible. Think of the American Revolution, the Civil Rights movement, the anti-apartheid movement in South Africa, and so on. Sometimes the recognized leader is young: Martin Luther King Jr. was 26 years old at the time of the Montgomery bus boycott. Young people have contributed importantly to major social justice struggles. My article "Young People's Contribution to Social Justice" catalogs some of these efforts.

Youth Activism Around the World

FIVE REASONS FOR THE CENTRALITY
OF LEADERSHIP DEVELOPMENT

YouthBuild has achieved remarkable success because it provides young people with so much of what they need to succeed: education, job skills, personal support, a positive peer community, caring staff, life skills, respect, safety, opportunity, a chance to make a difference, and a pathway to a brighter future. Though this full-time comprehensive approach is unusual among youth-serving organizations, YouthBuild's particular contribution is its emphasis on leadership development.

There are many organizations that prepare students for GEDs, that teach life skills, that engage in community service, that offer career counseling and job placement, that build affordable housing—all of which YouthBuild does well at its best. But no other program in this country does all of these simultaneously and combines them with the expectation that students will become leaders and provides the training for them to do so. This is what makes YouthBuild stand out, and this is where YouthBuild's potential is still mainly untapped.

YouthBuild is certainly about assisting young people in developing sustainable careers, advancing their educations, and creating a meaningful and healthy lives. At minimum these opportunities provide personal ladders out of poverty for young people. They are absolutely critical to the individual success of each YouthBuild graduate. But YouthBuild goes beyond individual success: it is also about creating pathways to opportunities to serve and lead beyond one's own life, and developing resources for the community—responsible, skilled leaders who can tackle the challenges that face us as a society.

Here are five key reasons why leadership development is central to YouthBuild.

1. Leadership calls forth higher potential in young people.
A list of basic needs and competencies for positive youth development includes a sense of belonging, self-worth, the ability to contribute, and citizenship. Consistently in YouthBuild we have noticed that the call to develop leadership in students counters two of the most persistent wounds to young people: a systematic invalidation of their intelligence, and exclusion from the decisions that affect their lives. Over time, when leadership development has been practiced well by a program, the benefits to the young people are observable. We see that students have an increased sense of self-worth, more skill at being able to engage and negotiate the wider world, a sense of being able to make a difference, a new identity as a leader, higher aspirations for themselves, the acceptance of greater levels of responsibility, a shedding of some levels of internalized oppression, and a growing desire to give back.

The YouthBuild short definition of good leadership—"taking responsibility to see that things go right for yourself, your family, your program, and your community"—itself incorporates the principles of youth development. Understood correctly and applied consistently, leadership development becomes a holistic youth-development approach. One reason that YouthBuild has chosen to call out leadership development is because much of the youth-development field has focused on the first two aspects of our definition—self and family, the traditional areas of social service. These are necessary building blocks, but not sufficient to develop the whole person. So in addition to the work required for personal development, we call on the young people to also take responsibility beyond themselves—for the program and the community. We expect them to engage in social change. This call for responsibility communicates respect for their caring and capacity to make positive changes in their environment. It reinforces their motivation to do the personal work. It appeals to their noblest aspirations for a decent world.

2. Leadership skills are sought by employers and colleges.
Lists of the skills and attitudes that employers and colleges seek in their candidates include the ability to work in teams, problem solving, flexibility, good judgment, and the ability to function effectively in a diverse environment. These are essentially leadership skills. They are also life skills but they show up on lists of leadership competencies, as in the US Department of Labor SCANS report on employee skills. So in YouthBuild, the more we emphasize such leadership skills the more we prepare young people for their postprogram placements in careers, registered apprenticeships, and colleges.

3. Emphasis on leadership leads to higher program outcomes.
Studies show that programs with a leadership-development approach tend to have higher program outcomes. Two short examples:

The Ford Foundation funded the Center for Innovation study of 20 youth organizations, half of which were traditional youth-development programs (after school programs, sports programs, and clubs), the other half were civic-engagement youth programs (youth organizing, advocacy, leadership). The study found that the young people in the youth leadership-oriented programs made greater youth development gains than the youth in the youth-development-only programs. This reinforces reason number 1 above.

Another example comes from a DOL-funded YouthBuild USA re-entry program for adjudicated youth in 34 YouthBuild programs from 2004 to 2007. Social Policy Research Associates (SPRA) conducted a study of this program and found that the programs with a well-functioning policy committee engaging youth in decision making had higher program outcomes across the board than those with no or weak policy committees. The relation was not necessarily causative, but was highly correlated.

This makes sense intuitively. If young people are respected, if their voice is heard, if they are invited into program decision making, then they are more likely to feel ownership in the program, attend regularly, and complete the program, which means they are more present to learn what the program has to offer, which means they tend to earn more GEDs, diplomas and credentials, learn more work skills, move in a more positive direction, give and receive more love and support, and realize more success in their post-program placements.

Furthermore, the decisions made by the program leadership are more likely to be appropriate and accurate if informed by the young people, and therefore the program as a whole will be more effective. The young people always have information that the staff do not have about what is really going on, and this information is useful in decision making. The takeaway here for YouthBuild directors is that paying attention to leadership development tends to boost program outcomes, which are so important for future funding as well as essential for the young people themselves.

4. Young people in leadership roles bring greater visibility and support to the program.

If young people are giving visitors the tours of the construction site, talking with the press, accompanying the director on fundraising visits, making presentations at the local Rotary Club, tutoring middle schoolers, and dialoguing with police about neighborhood safety, then the YouthBuild program receives more visibility, positive press coverage, and support. Even neighbors sitting on their porches, who knew some of the students in their earlier gang-banging days, see them walking through the neighborhood now with their tool belts and hard hats and feel pride. This visibility tends to make the wider community embrace YouthBuild, which in turn tends to lead to greater support, both in-kind and funding.

5. Leadership develops resources and human capital that helps the community tackle the issues of the day.

The previous four reasons are important in themselves, but the most compelling reason has to do with the world context in which Youth-Build sits.

We are in deep trouble on this earth. From many perspectives, it seems that the next 25 to 50 years are critical for the future of humankind. Some say it is a "breakdown or breakthrough" period, a stage that will "kill us or cure us." It is a time that calls upon us to accomplish at least the following six interrelated challenges if we are to break through:

1. Radically reduce world population growth before sheer numbers push the carrying capacity of the earth beyond repair.

2. Reverse the damage to the planet's life-support systems before the ozone, the ecosystems, the soil fertility, the forests, fisheries, and the water supplies are too far depleted to sustain life.

3. Reverse the dramatic climate changes before they melt the polar ice caps, flooding coastlines worldwide and changing wind, weather, and agricultural growing patterns.

4. Stop the spread of HIV/AIDS and other infectious diseases before they overwhelm our capacity to create antibodies and provide medical care.

5. Systematically dismantle the culture of violence and cultivate ways of peace, before conflicts morph into ongoing violence and wars, and possibly nuclear disaster.

6. Eliminate poverty and racism, and make the basics of a decent life available to all people before we are engulfed by the violence and terrorism that grows from the desperation, frustration, and hatreds that such current gross inequities foster.

These are all issues that directly affect poor communities that Youth-Build serves, both in the United States and internationally.

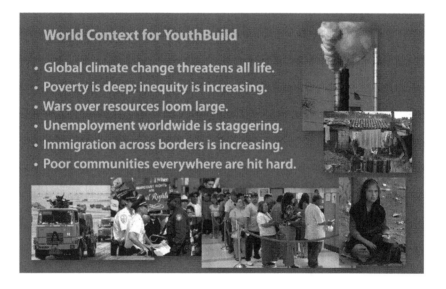

In my reading of the long course of events, it appears things evolve towards increasing cooperation and integration. For example, economic systems have come and gone, going through successive stages of slavery, feudalism, and now capitalism. Given enough time under normal conditions, it is possible that slow evolution would bring about a just and peaceful worldwide community. But because of the six crises listed above, there seems to be a new urgency about needing to promote transformation: most environmental scientists give it 50 years or less before the earth systems collapse if we continue on the present course. Poor people everywhere, including those in the United States, feel the negative impact of these huge forces but are rarely included in the solutions. Young people of all classes are excluded from decision making, especially low-income youth.

In addition, the gains made by young people in YouthBuild could be wiped out by these huge global forces. Helping young people learn a trade, get further education, and improve their individual lives is absolutely critical, but it is not enough in itself to protect them from these larger forces. If YouthBuild is only doing the social service, skill development part, it might be more like rearranging the deck chairs on the Titanic. We also need to put equal emphasis in YouthBuild on developing leaders who can become skilled, networked, organized, and active in tackling the issues of the day.

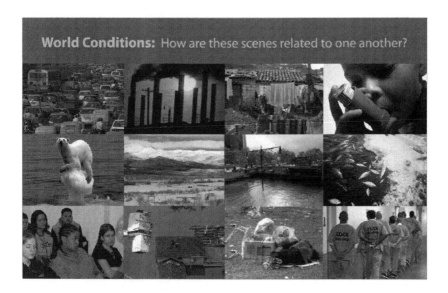

World Conditions: How are these scenes related to one another?

Since its beginnings, YouthBuild has been committed to developing the leadership capacity of young people from low-income communities. Given the conditions that YouthBuild provides, young people have reliably shown without a doubt that they have tremendous leadership ability, are eager to play a role in community development, have a deep desire to help change the conditions that cause poverty, and want to take responsibility for their lives, their families, their programs, and the wider world.

There is a fundamental need to develop young leaders at the fastest possible rate who are skilled and motivated to help handle the challenges that world conditions place before us.

As mentioned above, the world is facing multiple crises that call for leadership at all levels. Young people raised in poverty have experience, perspective, wisdom, and good ideas for helping to solve many problems. We need young people to be part of the human effort to meet the unprecedented challenges facing humankind if we are to have a fighting chance of surviving.

Helping to develop young leaders for these challenges is YouthBuild's North Star.

> **Five Key Reasons Leadership Development is Important**
> 1. Leadership calls forth higher potential in young people.
> 2. Leadership skills are sought by employers and colleges.
> 3. Emphasis on leadership leads to higher program outcomes.
> 4. Young people in leadership roles bring greater visibility and sup-port to the program.
> 5. Leadership develops resources for the community to help tackle the issues of the day.

LEADERSHIP DEVELOPMENT AT YOUTHBUILD ANYTOWN: A VISION

So now let us drop back to focus on leadership development in the YouthBuild program context. The following is a vision of what a well-developed, fully integrated leadership-development component might look like. No YouthBuild program to date has achieved all the elements described in this vision, but most everything described here has been used by some YouthBuild somewhere. Not all of these aspects of leadership development can be achieved in the first year or two. Like a house, a solid leadership-development program is built in stages. However, it is helpful to have a blueprint or vision to guide the stages of development. It is offered here as one picture of YouthBuild's potential as a leadership-development effort.

~

The fictitious YouthBuild Anytown program is six months into its third cycle. Last cycle's graduates helped the staff recruit and select the current participants. They selected people who seemed ready to make a positive change in their lives, who wanted to give back to the community, and who showed some leadership experience or potential.

During orientation, the new students were told that they were expected to be leaders in the program and in the community. To get into Youth-Build Anytown, each person had to agree in writing to register to vote if they were not prevented by legal constraints or religious convictions, to vote in every election during the program cycle, to attend the meetings of at least three different community organizations, to report back to the whole group about the community organizations, to serve on a leadership committee in the YouthBuild program, and to do two hours of community service per week in addition to housing construction. Each student took a preprogram leadership assessment survey to use as a benchmark against which to measure progress.

The staff and young people abide by a set of principles or core values that staff and youth from the first program cycle worked out together. The principles, as expressed in a daily pledge that the whole community recites each morning, are:

> We, the members of YouthBuild Anytown, pledge that we are working together
>
> - to improve and rebuild our community;
> - to relate to each other in cooperative ways;
> - to develop our potential as leaders;
> - to educate and improve ourselves and help others along the way;
> - to respect our peers, neighbors, and all life; and
> - to be part of a great movement for justice, equality, and peace.
>
> All this we will do with love and dignity.

From day one of the program, the young people learned that the first part of leadership is taking responsibility for oneself. The staff supported and challenged them to be on time, to attend every day, to refuse to make excuses, to be positive, to deal with anger constructively, to kick negative and self-destructive habits, to do the schoolwork, to take care of tools, to speak to others respectfully, and to develop other positive personal behaviors. Responsibility was taught as the foundation of good leadership.

After an orientation period, the policy committee was elected. The policy committee is a key governing center composed of six to eight elected students, the director, and a staff representative. The policy committee meets weekly. Students elected the most responsible of their peers for this job. The policy committee began with a weekend retreat where the committee members trained to prepare themselves for increasing responsibilities such as understanding the overall organizational structure, learning the role of the policy committee, and learning how to form an agenda, chair a meeting, read a budget, interview a job candidate, make consensus decisions, and use good group processes.

Because of this solid foundation, the policy committee was well respected by students and staff. It participated in disciplinary decisions, resolved conflict, hired staff, set program policies, and debated community issues. Two different non-policy committee members sat in on each meeting as observers. In this way, all YouthBuild members had contact with the committee. The committee used a standard meeting process, and in the beginning each member got a chance to chair a meeting.

Now there is a permanent youth chair who sets the agenda with the director and leads each meeting. The director and staff person are careful not to dominate. Another committee member takes notes and later checks them and posts them in the classroom or on the worksite. In the weekly community meeting, a member of the policy committee gives a verbal report and get feedback about the results of the meeting.

Leadership training and opportunities are not limited to those on the policy committee. All staff and students can discuss issues, set policies, and plan activities in monthly community meetings. Many young people have learned to lead small group discussions through these community meetings. Temporary committees form to take on special projects. A review committee handles discipline and grievances. All the participants and staff have been trained in mediation and conflict resolution and anyone can call for a mediation session with youth and staff mediators. There is also a community leadership committee for those who want to get involved in community action or advocacy beyond the YouthBuild program. The Anytown Community Leadership Committee members have given presentations in local public schools about subjects like staying in school and avoiding drugs. They have also set up a tutoring program, coached Little League, and sponsored a citywide youth conference.

Beyond these formal leadership committees, there are leadership jobs on the worksite and in the classroom. Young people serve as hosts by escorting visitors through the building and explaining the program. They take turns assisting the receptionist, answering phones, and doing some basic data-entry work.

The whole program reflects YouthBuild's concern for young leaders. There are prominent displays of quotes and pictures of leaders—from everyday leaders like the participants' mothers to public leaders like Nelson Mandela, Rosa Parks, Mahatma Gandhi, Colin Powell, Martin Luther King Jr., Cesar Chavez, Marian Wright Edelman, Sonia Sotomayor, Dorothy Stoneman, and many others. The YouthBuild definition of good leadership—*Good leadership is taking responsibility to make things go right for yourself, your family, the program, the community, and the planet.*—is posted in the classroom and on the worksite. The classroom teacher uses a leadership curriculum that teaches basic skills while covering topics like the history of the community and its peoples, social change movements and their leaders, theories of change, public speaking, writing skills, and community organizing methods.

The program uses leadership *competencies*, a specific set of practical skills and information development by YouthBuild USA, which each participant is required to master by graduation. Leadership competencies include how to keep a weekly schedule calendar, set a personal budget, listen well, take good notes, lead a small group discussion, explain helpful group process techniques, use the Internet to do research and find information, and access local government.

Weekly leadership workshops are held every Friday morning. Some of these workshops teach a leadership competency. Others feature an outside speaker, community leader, or local public official. Still others get the YouthBuild members, staff, and young people to explore issues of cultural diversity in an ongoing effort to increase understanding and combat oppression. They have classes on current political and economic issues to sharpen their critical thinking skills and help them form useful analyses. These kinds of experiences give the participants a larger world view. Some of YouthBuild young people write a regular column in the community newspaper on the world from a youth perspective, or appear on a local cable television show.

YouthBuild Anytown ensures that the youth perspective extends beyond its own program boundaries. The director regularly takes participants and graduates to visit foundations and government agencies in order to assist with fundraising. Young people speak to the press and testify at city council meetings. Staff often take young people with them to their own community meetings. Several young people attend a YouthBuild national youth conference in Washington, DC, attend leadership workshops, and meet youth from YouthBuild programs all over the country.

However, no program always runs smoothly. There are conflicts, flare-ups, contract violations, staff and student disrespect, negative behavior, and occasional terminations. Even outstanding leaders struggle with such issues as acting responsibly on the policy committee, attending regularly, following up on promises made, resisting peer pressure to act out in the classroom, and feeling guilt about leaving behind friends from their previous street life. Personal crises sometimes cause a young person to slip backwards. However, the program has trained the young people and staff in restorative practices and nonviolent communication as tools for handling such stressful times.

Everyone is continually reminded of the principles as guiding ideas. The students take responsibility for handling common negative behavior among themselves. The review committee formally handles grievances or serious violations. The counselors teach methods of anger management and conflict resolution. The program uses peer counseling and support groups to gradually increase trust levels, allow for caring and healing, build community, improve listening skills, and challenge negative behavior and attitudes. The program recognizes that further leadership development is often blocked by internalized attitudes and stored emotional pain collected over a lifetime. Personal development and leadership development go hand in hand. The staff expects participants to do both.

The key component of YouthBuild Anytown's leadership program is the commitment of the director and staff. The director, with the backing of the board, sees the program as a training ground for solid citizens and community leaders. The director has hired and trained a staff who view young people as leaders helping to run the program rather than as clients needing services. Over the past two years, she has also fired a staff person who could not respect young people in practice, who was adultist. (See my article "Understanding Adultism" for a clear explanation of this important and little-understood concept.) The director has helped the staff build a vision for leadership development. There are ongoing, regular staff-development trainings in leadership development. The program has determined desired outcomes of its leadership-development component.

As a result, each staff member sees himself as a leadership developer, whether through teaching, counseling, or construction training. Each staff member sets leadership goals and objectives for which he or she is held responsible. In addition to standard classroom curricula, staff encourage students to use art, videos, and other creative communication to learn and express their leadership. Twice a year the staff does a formal written and verbal evaluation of the leadership program. In addition, the staff position of leadership developer is responsible for scheduling workshops, lining up speakers, planning leadership retreats; keeping track of leadership competencies, supporting the policy committee and other youth committees, and helping other staff keep leadership development high on their agendas.

As a result of this approach, most participants graduate with confidence in themselves and their ability to change their lives and create a positive future. They have a knowledge base and a toolkit of leadership skills. They have had a year of various leadership experiences. They have seen the connection between their own neighborhoods and the wider world.

Many graduates are now members of their children's schools' PTAs and other community organizations. Some serve on community boards and keep informed about politics and public issues. These graduates vote regularly. One graduate was hired by the YouthBuild program as an assistant construction trainer. Two graduates are on YouthBuild Anytown's board. Another graduate plans to run for the local school committee. The majority of graduates are serving as role models for those around them because they are positive people who are responsible parents, steady job holders, and mentors for younger people.

Many graduates are in college. Some have become or aspire to become youth workers, AIDS counselors, or community leaders. Most stay active with YouthBuild Anytown's alumni club and Graduate Program, which provide job and personal counseling, further educational opportunities, positive social activities, and ongoing leadership roles. The community views YouthBuild Anytown as a real resource. Employers are eager to hire graduates because of their good work skills and responsible attitudes. Consequently, local foundations, churches, agencies, businesses, and media consider YouthBuild Anytown a community treasure and give it support in many forms.

THE LONG VIEW—20 YEARS FROM NOW

Let us take the long view. As of now, there are about 10,000 young people who participate in YouthBuild in the United States each year. Imagine it is 20 years from now. Assuming the current 7,000 to 10,000 YouthBuild graduates per year, in 20 years there are 200,000 graduates. This is a sizable force for good. Over these past 20 years, the Youth-Build network has intentionally and systematically supported, nurtured, trained, networked, mobilized, and organized graduate leaders along the lines of the vision sketched in the last section. As a result, a substantial number of graduates are deeply engaged in their communities. They belong to their PTAs, local unions, and church organizations. Most have attained a postsecondary college degree or certification. Some have been elected to school committees, city planning boards, or city and state offices.

Additionally, many graduates have created successful community businesses. They run day-care centers, home-repair services, taxi companies, construction companies, beauty parlors and health clubs, tutoring services, medical and dental clinics, dance schools, and so on. They employ community folks, which supports community asset development. YouthBuild graduates are known for being respectful, responsible, reliable, and resourceful. They are sought out as facilitators, mediators, and strategic allies. They chair or sit on many of the influential community boards. They bring unity, cohesion, and collaboration toward common visions. Over many years, they organized to create quality education for the children, safe neighborhoods for everyone, a green community that cares for the earth, just treatment for residents, cooperative economic development, living wage for workers, affordable quality health care for all, and a vibrant, successful community, They are decision makers who help shape what happens in the community. One of the best parts is that their children are watching them care about the community and the world. This modeling is worth its weight in gold for the development of responsible future leaders.

This vision is not just fanciful. It sketches some conditions of leadership that will be needed to bring us through the impending challenges facing us. The exact shape of the future is unknown. But one thing is certain. No matter what happens, it requires leadership. (To get a sense of the fruits of YouthBuild's long-term investment in youth leadership, see *Pathways into Leadership: A Study of YouthBuild Graduates.*)

THREE KEY LEADERSHIP PRACTICES

Vision is one thing. Bringing it to life is another. Over the years Youth-Build USA has written handbooks and offered hundreds of workshops on various ways to implement leadership development. Plenty of information can be found in the various publications and articles listed in resources section at the end of this book. For now, I want to touch on three key practices of leadership development that form the basis of a sound leadership approach.

First, some definitions. YouthBuild USA has used this definition of good leadership since the early 1990s. Originally, it was the upper four circles, but with our entry into the green-building arena and growing awareness of the environmental crisis, we added "planet" to the definition.

Leadership: Good leadership is taking responsibility to see that things go right for my life, my family, my program, my community, and the planet.

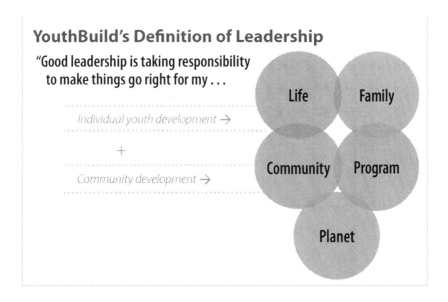

YouthBuild's Definition of Leadership

"Good leadership is taking responsibility to make things go right for my . . .

Individual youth development →

+

Community development →

Life

Family

Community

Program

Planet

Leadership development: If taking responsibility is the key part of our definition of leadership, then leadership development is expanding the capacity to take increasing responsibility.

The circles in the illustration above are intersecting and interactive to show that leadership *development* is not a linear process, as in: first you get your life together, then you can care for your family, then you can take more responsibility for your YouthBuild program, and then you can contribute to your community. Rather, our experience is that leadership development is more interrelated and simultaneous. For example:

- The mayor visits the program. The policy committee chairperson is asked to write a thank-you letter and so needs to learn the proper form of a business letter.

- When young people come to Washington, DC, each year for the annual Conference of Young Leaders they visit Capitol Hill and meet with members of Congress and their aides to advocate for the federal YouthBuild appropriation. They experience making a difference. This motivates them to learn more about how government works.

- Learning good group processes in the program helps have better family meetings.

- Accompanying the director to a Rotary Club meeting motivates a student to learn public speaking.

And so on.

The chart below shows eight elements of a holistic leadership-development program embedded in the vision above.

Components of a Strong Leadership Approach
(LD = Leadership Development)

What is LD

Youth decision making

Benefits of LD

LD in all components

Vision for LD

LD competencies

Staff LD roles

LD culture

In the preceding sections, we have talked a little about the definition, benefits, vision, and culture of leadership development. Now we will focus in on the three elements on the left-hand side: leadership development in all components, a program policy committee as a structured form for youth decision making, and leadership competencies to teach and measure skills. There is more detail on these three sections because if a program focuses on just these three practices along the lines below, it will have a solid leadership-development program.

LEADERSHIP DEVELOPMENT INTEGRATED THROUGHOUT THE PROGRAM

YouthBuild directors have told me that some staff say, "You mean I have to do leadership development on top of my job?!" Or, "My funders don't care about leadership development; they just care about outcomes." Or, "We do leadership development in a workshop every Friday afternoon." To me, these are misunderstandings of leadership development. For leadership development to succeed, it needs to be thoroughly embedded throughout the program components and operations.

To reiterate something I mentioned in the chapter on staff cohesion, where possible I would hire staff who were leaders in their own right. For example, a construction manager who was active in the local carpenters union, a teacher who was part of a teacher community, a counselor who was active in local community affairs, a career counselor who belonged to the local business roundtable, a leadership developer who had worked in political campaigns, and so on. I would be clear with staff that their second job, after loving young people, was to develop their leadership potential. I would want staff to take young people with them to meetings of their trade unions, business associations, and community-action groups. I would expect staff to expose young people to the larger community and wider issues than they might have had contact with so far, and introduce them to community leaders. I would expect staff to be concerned about world affairs and actively bring current events into their discussions with young people as part of raising their awareness about the world. I would hire staff who had a humanistic and positive vision for society, their own version of Dr. King's "beloved community." The following charts give some examples of how programs have built leadership development into all components. Other ideas can be found in the *Leadership Development at a YouthBuild Program Handbook.*

Leadership Development in **Classroom Structure**

Young people:

- Help decide classroom activities
- Are responsible for finishing and correcting their own work
- Have opportunities to work in teams
- Teach each other
- Rotate leadership jobs in the classroom
- Participate in evaluating teachers

Leadership Development in the **Classroom Content**

Young people:

- Research topics of community concern or current event
- Make presentations to the class or entire program on a community issue
- Participate in formal debate
- Write letters to editors or Congresspeople
- Visit and dialogue with public officials
- Use *Blueprint for Democracy*, a civic-engagement curriculum from YouthBuild USA
- Study the history and culture of the racial and ethnic groups that students belong to
- Study the movements of poor people fighting for equal opportunity
- Learn about the climate crisis and become green leaders

Leadership Development at **the Construction Worksite**

Young people:

- Rotate leadership roles (for example, act in turn as crew chief, safety coordinator, tool captain, site steward (responsible for calling for breaks, cleanup, attendance), or as the person who makes supply store runs or takes photographs to document work)
- Attend contract negotiations or go to city hall to pull permits
- Help plan, estimate materials for, and create schedule for work projects
- Conduct tours for site visitors
- Learn why green building is important, become leaders on environmental issues
- Evaluate the construction staff and each other

Leadership Development in the **Counseling Component**

Young people strengthen their leadership by:

- Learning to lead discussion groups
- Learning to counsel peers
- Practicing peer mediation and conflict resolution
- Exploring cultural-diversity issues
- Making individual leadership-development and life plans
- Learning to better navigate the external world

Leadership Development in **Program Operations**

Young people:

- Are assumed and expected to be leaders
- Help make program rules and discipline policies
- Accompany the director on fundraising visits
- Take turns being office receptionist, answering phones, and doing data entry
- Lead morning meetings and program events
- Show visitors around, handle press interviews
- Care for the physical environment: recycle used materials, conserve energy, care for equipment

Leadership Development in the **Wider Community**

Young people:

- Choose and organize community service
- Offer tutoring, computer skills, and mentoring to younger children
- Bring presentations about staying in school and off drugs to local schools
- Bring to policy makers presentations about needed changes
- Organize and host community youth conferences

PROGRAM POLICY COMMITTEE

The second key leadership-development practice in YouthBuild is to create and sustain an effective program policy committee. The most comprehensive explanation can be found in the *YouthBuild Policy Committee Handbook*. This handbook is a synthesis of the best practices from the first 10 years of doing policy committees across the network. Directors have told me repeatedly that if they follow that handbook, they tend to have successful policy committees, so it comes highly recommended. For the purposes of this book, we will summarize the main points.

Policy committee meeting: What do you notice?

The photo above is of a policy committee meeting at Young Detroit Builders YouthBuild program. The members are engaged, organized, purposeful, student-led. They are meeting in what looks to be an orderly private space with natural light, plants, and meeting equipment. The notebook in front of them is actually the *YouthBuild Policy Committee Handbook*.

There are many potential benefits of having young people this involved in this key decision-making committee. The policy committee can:

- Be the place where the most intense leadership development takes place

- Help the young people feel more ownership of the program

- Become a group that sets the tone for the entire program

- Present good solutions to pressing problems

- Be a source of good thinking and support for the decisions that weigh on the director

- Make the program more responsive to the needs and successes of the young people

- Assist the young people in counteracting the experience of having often been excluded from decisions that affect them

- Allow young people to learn how an organization works

- Be the training ground for young leaders who can take what they learn on the policy committee and apply it out in the world.

- Help young people learn leadership skills sought by employers and colleges

- Help improve program attendance, retention, and outcomes because young people feel more ownership.

This level of functioning does not happen by accident. There are six key ingredients that make a policy committee successful, as outlined in the chart below.

Key Ingredients for Success of Policy Committee

1. Solid preparation
2. Structured respect
3. Serious business
4. Serious training
5. Effective group process
6. Clear accountability and relationships

1. **Solid preparation.** The first ingredient requires the director to formulate the structure and scope of powers and responsibilities and to make sure the staff understand and support it. Without staff understanding and buy-in, the policy committee is not likely to gain the support of and be respected by staff. Typically a policy committee includes the director and one staff representative so the staff can be included but not be dominant. The written description should cover the range of things from what is expected and required of policy committee members to what they can and cannot decide, whether there is pizza at the meetings, and whether it is a paid or voluntary activity. Another piece of preparation is to hold an effective election process that teaches leadership concepts. It is best to wait until four to six weeks into the program cycle to hold the election. By that time, the young people will know who is for real and will tend to elect more serious leaders, and not just the popular students. However, for the period before the election, it is best to create a temporary advisory committee that meets regularly with the director. This lets students know that their voice is important right from the beginning. In the run-up to the election, if I were the director I would also be planting seeds in the minds of students whom I thought might be

solid policy-committee candidates. To a quiet leader I might say something like, "Jazzie, I have noticed that you have good ideas and listen well. Have you considered running for the policy committee?" (See the *YouthBuild Policy Committee Handbook* for the detailed election process.)

Key ingredients for success of policy committee

1. Solid preparation

- Staff agreement on
  - Structure
  - Responsibilities
  - Criteria for members
  - Procedures
- Training
- Staff training on policy committees
- Effective election process

---

2. **Structured respect.** The second ingredient for a successful policy committee is what I call *structured respect*—that is, elements built in that communicate respect. The most critical one is that the director or executive director is part of the committee and meets with the young people consistently. Why? For several reasons. One is that although the policy committee without the director could make good decisions, they still would need to take the decisions to the director, so it is more efficient to include the person with the most organizational power in the process from the beginning. The second reason is that most young people, left to themselves, will think about issues most relevant to themselves. This is as it should be. It is the job of the director to bring to the young folks issues that the director is aware of, and ask young people to think on these larger agency issues. This is leadership development. Thirdly, the director needs to be tuned in and listening to the young people because they always know more about what's

really going on than the director. By listening well, the director's decisions will be better. Finally, the message to the students that is given by the consistent presence of the director is one of profound respect: *You are worth my time, your ideas are important to me, you are important in this organization.*

Key ingredients for success of policy committee

2. Structured respect

Examples:

- Holding private regularly scheduled meetings
- Including director of program in meetings
- Preparing an agenda
- Identifying the supports members will need to ensure success in their roles
- Determining the staffing, financial, and time resources needed

---

3. **Serious business.** One important step is to make sure decision-making responsibilities are substantial. When I was a student leader in high school, we were allowed to make decisions like whether to have a Coke machine or a Pepsi machine in the cafeteria. Pretty low level, if not downright insulting. In YouthBuild, we invite young people to help make decisions on key issues, not just how to punish other students who break rules or organize entertaining activities for the class, but core policies affecting the program, as outlined in the chart below.

Key ingredients for success of policy committee

Examples of policy committee responsibilities

- Consult on program design
- Select community-service projects
- Mediate conflicts
- Propose development policy recommendations to elected officials
- Review annual budget
- Plan events
- Participate in hiring of staff
- Recommend and review policy changes

---

4. **Serious training.** Young people usually don't come into Youth-Build knowing how to form an agenda, read a budget, interview staff candidates, or run an effective meeting. The job of the director is to take seriously the skill development of policy committee members by providing adequate training and preparation that allows them to function well as committee members.

Key ingredients for success of policy committee

4. Serious Training

Examples of trainings . . . How to:

- Form an agenda
- Lead a productive meeting
- Use consensus decision making
- Read a budget
- Listen well
- Conduct interviews

---

5. *Effective group process.* Young people, like all of us, want to be part of a productive, well-run meeting where their participation is encouraged and their ideas valued. So it is important to pay

attention to using good process in the meetings. If the director is not the best process person, invite the staff person who is good on process to model good process until all policy committee members have internalized it and it becomes the normal way of operating. (For descriptions of some of these effective group-process methods, see my article "Creating Conditions for Good Learning, Thinking, and Decision Making.")

Key ingredients for success of policy committee

5. Effective group process

Some elements:

- Solid meeting structure
- Rotating chairpersons
- Facilitation skills
- Respectful listening
- Arguing another's point

---

6. **Clear accountability and relationships.** The members of the policy committee need to have structured ways of reporting out to their peers and getting feedback. Otherwise they can get isolated and undermined. Also, the director needs to keep building the group and resolving any little conflicts between members before the conflicts get blown out of proportion.

Key ingredients for success of policy committee

6. Clear accountability and relationships

- Set clear standards for conduct
- Understand the role of the director and staff on policy committee
- Encourage regular report-outs to all students
- Build relationships intentionally
- Resolve conflicts well
- Have fun!

COMMON MISTAKES TO AVOID
IN DEVELOPING A POLICY COMMITTEE

If young people start skipping policy committee meetings reduce their involvement, act bored and unengaged in the meetings, start to feel separate from the rest of the students, or show other signs of dysfunction, then one or more of these common mistakes are happening, and the situation needs attention.

- **Unwillingness to share power.** Sometimes the director or staff is not willing to let young people make important decisions. I once had a conversation with a YouthBuild director new in her position who told me that "these young people made bad decisions in their lives, and that's why they are here. I'm not going to let them make bad decisions for my program!" She has since adopted a new perspective and has a policy committee.

- **Director dominates policy committee.** Sometimes the director or staff representative does all the talking, runs the meetings, and doesn't listen to young people. Soon, the students will stop coming.

- **Director is too hands-off.** In the opposite direction, we've seen directors give very little guidance or training for fear of interfering with youth decisions. This is a mistaken view of the director's role, which is to set the tone and bring important issues and information, and to ensure good process for the group.

- **Tasks not substantial.** If the scope of responsibility is small, or if the director does not use the group to deliberate on important issues that the director is facing, then young people will soon feel it's not worth their time and will check out.

- **Not enough training.** Without proper training, the policy committee will be less prepared to handle substantive issues. They won't know how to read a budget or interview candidates properly. This leads to discouragement.

- **Poor group process.** If meetings are unstructured and debate is chaotic or full of conflict, or if members don't feel listened to or valued, they will leave. Here it is worth mentioning that the process must include teaching the young people to handle sensitive information with discretion and practice confidentiality.

- **Poor follow-up.** If the director doesn't act on policy committee decisions, or members don't do what they have agreed to do, then members and the other students rightly conclude that the policy committee is not for real. They will check out.

- **Policy committee gets isolated from other students.** Sometimes not enough thought is given to how the policy committee relates to the rest of the young people. For example, there are few times when the policy committee asks for input or reports out to whole program; or, policy committee members come to think they are "all that," something special and make other students feel excluded; or, policy committee makes policy decisions that staff can't support. If these kinds of things happen, the other students or staff will undermine the policy committee.

Key ingredients for success of policy committee

Common mistakes to avoid with policy committee
- Unwillingness to share power
- Director dominates policy committee
- Director is too hands-off
- Tasks not substantial
- Not enough training
- Poor group process
- Poor follow-up
- Committee gets isolated from other students

But if you avoid those mistakes and pay attention to the development of the policy committee, the scene below is more what you will get. Well worth the effort.

LEADERSHIP COMPETENCIES

The third key leadership-development practice, along with integrating leadership into every component and developing an effective policy committee, is the use of a set of leadership competencies. Just as there are competencies that are taught and learned on the construction site and competencies that are required to pass the high school equivalency test or achieve a high school diploma, there are leadership skills and competencies that can be taught and learned in a YouthBuild program.

In the YouthBuild context, leadership means young people take responsibility to make sure things go right for themselves, their families, and their communities. Leadership development is also key to helping YouthBuild students work toward their learning and career goals and success in their postprogram placements. Many of the same competencies necessary for students to become leaders in their families, programs, and communities are also the kinds of foundational skills sought by employers and needed to succeed in higher education. When planning leadership development activities and measuring leadership development among program participants, YouthBuild programs should be mindful of the intersections between leadership development, higher education, and workplace competencies.

YouthBuild USA, with input from YouthBuild directors, staff, and graduates, has developed a set of 23 Leadership Competencies. The competencies are in three categories:

- Personal leadership skills and knowledge
- Small group leadership skills and knowledge
- Community leadership skills and knowledge.

Each competency has an example of a benchmark against which a program could assess progress if a participant is attaining the competency. Benchmarks need to be customized to each program, so these are simply illustrative. In addition, as is evident from the sample benchmarks below, activities across the program should provide opportunities for participants to work toward competency attainment. For example, some of the benchmarks are the results of classroom writing activities, some would be achieved in consultation with the counselor or career developer, and some can be achieved on the construction worksite. In this document, we highlight ways in which these activities might be directly linked to career development and preparation for college. Lastly, we suggest that a program set standards for completion, for example, "To graduate, a student must satisfactorily attain 80 percent of these leadership competencies." The student is then awarded a certificate, which can be added to his or her résumé or portfolio.

On the next page begins a listing of the 23 Leadership Competencies. You will notice that these are not rocket science. There are other important competencies that could have been included. We chose this set because it was thought that they could be taught and learned in the context of a 9- to 12-month YouthBuild cycle. The point is to make leadership skills concrete, relevant to the lives of young people, and measurable. YouthBuild USA offers a sample template for tracking and measuring student achievement of the competencies.

Personal Leadership Skills and Knowledge

Basic competencies

Sample benchmarks

1. Schedule

Keeps and uses a weekly schedule and calendar.

General Leadership
Spot checks of calendar and weekly schedule show up-to-date program activities and appointments.

Career Ready
Maintains a calendar with work site, internship and job placement schedules.

Postsecondary Ready
Maintains an up-to-date calendar for short- and long-term scheduling for all classroom assignments.

2. E-mail

Has and uses an e-mail account, Facebook page, or other social media networking platform.

General Leadership
Consistently replies to weekly e-mails from program director.

Career Ready
Writes professional e-mails, and uses e-mail for job applications when appropriate. (Professional user name should be part of basic competency.)

Postsecondary Ready
Can complete, save, discuss, and submit coursework electronically.

3. Goal setting

Sets and makes progress towards personal development goals. Understands value of long-term goals and deferred gratification. Can use self-evaluation and feedback from others to evaluate progress toward goals.

General Leadership
Individual development plan lists goals and records regular self-assessment of progress toward goals, with modifications as needed. Demonstrates ability to ask for feedback about goals.

Career Ready
Individual development plan includes career and education plans with clear and achievable goals.

Personal Leadership Skills and Knowledge

Basic competencies	Sample benchmarks
4. Emotional control Handles own anger, frustration, disappointments, and reactions to personal or societal disrespect and mistreatment in a constructive way.	***General Leadership*** Instances of improvement in managing anger or disappointment constructively are recognized by staff or fellow students and are recorded in case notes. ***Career Ready*** Instances are noted in which the student's communicates effectively and in a productive manner about frustrations on the work site and in the classroom.
5. Financial literacy Has basic financial literacy skills: pays bills, saves money, makes and uses a personal budget.	***General Leadership*** Budget and biweekly reconciliations are turned in. ***Postsecondary Ready*** Creates a budget for financing postsecondary education expenses, considering financial aid and living expenses. Keeps this budget up-to-date as plans for postsecondary education progress.
6. Note taking Takes useful notes in class, in meetings, and on the work site.	***General Leadership*** Written work site safety tips, based on notes taken on work site, potentially to be used for program poster. ***Career Ready*** Written notes about career paths from career presentations, job shadowing, and informational interviews are kept in a journal or used in group discussions and presentations. ***Postsecondary Ready*** Takes well-organized notes which capture key learning concepts and demonstrate understanding of content.

Personal Leadership Skills and Knowledge

Basic competencies	Sample benchmarks
7. Researching Can find information through researching.	***General Leadership*** Researches topics of interest using a variety of sources such as the Internet and the library. Is able to evaluate those sources. ***Career Ready*** Uses information found through research to prepare presentation on a career pathway that matches the student's interests and local labor-market demand. ***Postsecondary Ready*** Can distinguish between the validity of various research sources and use legitimate resources to construct a research paper.
8. Personal values Can articulate how own personal values and beliefs affect his or her decision.	***General Leadership*** Writes essay about how a personal value has affected his or her life choices. ***Career Ready*** Journal entry describing how personal values and beliefs might influence the student's career choice.
9. Support network Seeks and takes advantage of a positive support network and has someone to turn to during times of need.	***General Leadership*** Develops a mentor; creates a strong circle of friends; associates with positive people.
10. Community resources Can identify and secure community resources and supports to help meet their own needs.	***General Leadership*** Creates contact list of important community resources, any self- reports of using these resources are recorded in case notes. ***Career Ready*** Can identify community resources for finding a job and developing career skills (such as Career OneStop and the nearest community college). ***Postsecondary ready*** Proactively approaches instructors, professors, and counselors for additional understanding and support.

Small Group Leadership Skills and Knowledge

Basic competencies	Sample benchmarks
11. Define leadership Can define the functions, skills, attitudes, and qualities of good leaders.	***General Leadership*** Writes essay, short story, or poem that describes the functions, skills, attitudes, and qualities of a good leader. ***Career Ready*** Writes essay, short story, or poem that describes how the qualities that make someone a good leader apply in a variety of situations, including the workplace. ***Postsecondary Ready*** Completes research paper on the role of a leader in the students' community or a historical leader who impacted the young persons' life experience.
12. Listening Listens well to others in class, in meetings, and on the work site.	***General Leadership*** Participates effectively in class discussions, listening respectfully to the opinions of others. ***Career Ready*** On the work site and during group projects, is able to take on different roles as part of the team—being a listener when necessary. Exhibits tact and diplomacy, showing sensitivity to the thoughts of others. ***Postsecondary Ready*** Can actively participate in and lead group academic projects.
13. Public speaking Can prepare for and give a presentation in front of a group.	***General Leadership*** Delivers a written presentation about an issue in the community that is important to the student. ***Career Ready*** Practices speaking to community leaders at city hall meetings, developing professional communication and presentation skills. Presentation on a career track and videotape of presentation. ***Postsecondary Ready*** Presents projects from academic portfolio to peers, educators, community, and workforce partners.

Small Group Leadership Skills and Knowledge

Basic competencies	Sample benchmarks
14. Group process Can explain and participate in a variety of group process methods such as brainstorming, small group sharing, equal time go-arounds, and appreciations.	*General Leadership* Is observed facilitating a brainstorming session, or participates in appreciating peers; demonstrates use of other group processes.
15. Small group meetings Can lead an effective small group discussion, or follow an agenda, or reach a decision.	*General Leadership* Leads an effective small group discussion about an in-class assignment. Observed facilitating a meeting agenda or making a decision. *Career Ready* Works as a team to develop a set of priorities for improving relationships on the work site, helping to identify team goals, resolve conflicts, and reach consensus. *Postsecondary Ready* Leads an effective small-group discussion about strategies for succeeding in postsecondary education (possibly a discussion to include alumni), making sure that everyone's opinions are heard and taken into consideration.

Community Leadership Skills And Knowledge

Basic competencies	Sample Benchmarks
16. Knowledge of government Can explain the basics of how local, state, and national governments work.	*General Leadership* Creates poster with explanations; presents to elementary school students.
17. Voting If eligible, is registered to vote and knows how to vote.	*General Leadership* Copy of completed voter registration form; votes in program election using simulated voting system.

Community Leadership Skills And Knowledge

Basic competencies	Sample Benchmarks
18. Using media to raise public concern Can write a letter to the editor or local official to bring attention to a concern, or can post a blog or launch a Facebook campaign.	*General Leadership* Completes letter to the editor. *Career Ready* Is able to write a clear, coherent, persuasive document and communicate ideas, opinions, and concerns clearly and coherently.
19. Research issues Can research and advocate for issues important to him or her.	*General Leadership* Writes proposal for a way to improve the program. *Career and Postsecondary Ready* Writes proposal for way to improve the work site or his or her roles at the work site. Is able to identify problems, consider alternatives and determine possible solutions. Effectively locates, gathers, and organizes relevant information.
20. Service Can identify opportunities to serve the community.	*General Leadership* Identifies potential projects, and organizes and executes a realistic plan, evaluating the plan as it progresses, making adaptations as necessary. *Postsecondary Ready* Participates in and leads service-learning projects with the efficacy to select projects with community value and connections to classroom learning goals

Community Leadership Skills And Knowledge

Basic competencies	Sample Benchmarks
21. Cultural competence Demonstrates respect for cultural differences among peers and in the community. Understands and effectively communicates terms of oppression (such as racism, sexism, adultism).	*General Leadership* is observed by staff as having a basic understanding of oppression; has journal entry describing personal experience of oppression; has a working vocabulary of the different dimension of diversity; demonstrates knowledge through writings, role plays, and conversations. *Career Ready* Is able to discuss and acknowledge cultural differences respectfully. Writes a journal entry about how cultural differences could affect working relationships and how best to address issues as they arise.
22. Community mapping Can map assets and key influential organizations, people and forces in the community.	*General Leadership* Creates poster map of community. *Career Ready* Locates and interviews career development centers, OneStop center, and career training resources.
23. Organizing events Can plan, organize and implement a program activity or event.	*General Leadership* Writes plan for program event and writes post-program evaluation. *Career and Postsecondary Ready* Plans and implements a career and postsecondary development event—for example, a pizza party with alumni who are currently working towards postsecondary education credentials.

7

Education

*I*n this book we have been viewing YouthBuild as part of a broad movement aimed at eliminating poverty and creating a caring society, and seeing that YouthBuild's main contribution to this effort is the development of young leaders skilled and inspired to help make this a reality. YouthBuild's North Star. To accelerate the development of young leaders, we have examined several key areas in Youth-Build that need to be improved or deepened. Chapter 3 sketched a holistic vision of YouthBuild at a robust integrated level of development. Chapter 4 focused on the need for a coherent set of core values and a program culture where everything speaks those values. Chapter 5 scoped out the qualities and abilities needed in the staff to support the core values and culture. And Chapter 6 made the case for putting leadership development at the center of the program.

In this chapter I want to look at the role of education in supporting YouthBuild as a leadership development and movement-building effort toward creating the "beloved community," to use Martin Luther King Jr.'s lovely phrase. In addition to being a longtime YouthBuild veteran, I do have education credentials that help shape my ideas. Teaching was my first career, and everything I've done since has grown out of my early work in education. I have a master's degree in education from Stanford University, and have taught at the elementary, junior high, high school, and college levels; in public schools, storefront parent-controlled schools, a teacher's college, and in neighborhood organizations. I have shepherded my own children through various levels of the educational system, including home schooling. While I am not deeply versed in the latest educational thinking, theory, or movements, I still have a keen interest in education and still consider myself an educator.

SOME ASSUMPTIONS ABOUT EDUCATION AND THE LEARNING PROCESS

Before talking about the role of education in YouthBuild, I would like to state a few of my assumptions:

- Education is a vital key to youth transformation and societal transformation.

- In contrast to commonly held views, the unstated and unconscious purpose of public education (K–12), and much of college, is to condition people to take their places in the current economic system.

- Most of what is called "education" in our society insults the intelligence of learners because it represses creativity and deep thinking. There are many excellent teachers and school leaders who succeed at creating transformative classrooms and schools, but these are exceptions in a system that dulls the natural intelligence of young people.

- Critical thinking, holistic learning, social-emotional learning, and leadership development should be at the heart of a YouthBuild education.

- YouthBuild has the potential of being a positive force in meaningful and real education reform.

Since, in YouthBuild, we want to maximize the learning of the young people, whether it is in the classroom, on the worksite, or in a meeting or workshop, it is good to remember some basic information about the nature of the way people learn. I present a few salient points, culled from research and my own training and experience. You may not agree with each of these, but it is important for me to be transparent, since this set of ideas, along with those listed above, shape my recommendations for education in YouthBuild.

Learning is easy and natural to human beings. This is certainly obvious in babies and young children who learn a mile a minute. This may be hard to see in the students who come to YouthBuild because their natural learning ability has often been severely damaged by years of dull schooling and by harsh, mind-numbing environments. To learn well, a person must not be distressed, either by present conditions or past hurts. A person cannot learn well if he or she is hurting, overtired, depressed, frightened, embarrassed, ashamed, angry, confused, or bored. Sometimes you have to deal with what is upsetting the learner before he or she can learn effectively. There is the whole field of social and emotional learning that has grown up to address this. Our Youth-Build classrooms, schools, and programs help young people overcome their blocks and recover their innate ability to learn.

We know some conditions that enhance learning. People learn best when they feel good and feel good about themselves, can heal the hurts that interfere with learning, feel liked and approved, have consistent learning successes, have choices in what to learn, have a context of familiar information on which to hang new information, hear information repeated in new and varied ways, have a chance to tell someone what they just learned, have information presented in small doses to process it well, and are in a learning environment that is supportive and positive.

Ideally, learning itself is motive enough. Watch a baby or young child and you'll see unlimited curiosity and nonstop learning. Unfortunately, most young people get heavily conditioned to seek outside validation and sometimes motivation through tests, examinations, grades, and warnings. By and large, these interfere profoundly with a learner's natural ability and desire to learn. They create tensions, anxiety, competition, insecurities, and doubts in learners. Since the young people in YouthBuild will be tested for the high school equivalency or high school diploma, we have to prepare them for succeeding at test taking. But in YouthBuild we need to view testing as a strategy or method, not a goal or the measure of a person.

A good learning situation makes it impossible for the learner to feel like a failure. Not succeeding is data for learning. Avoid all occasions in which a learner would feel stupid, embarrassed, and humiliated. Design questions, assignments, and projects to allow the learner to feel successful, smart, and creative.

Considering everything bearing down on the young people, they are always doing the best that they can and so do not deserve blame or criticism. Since most YouthBuild young people have received heaps of invalidation, they need lots approval and praise to counteract that negative conditioning. This awareness implies some practices that are common for YouthBuild staff, and especially instructors, teachers, and trainers. They cannot overdo praise and approval. They should encourage students to ask questions, ask questions, ask questions; never scold, ridicule, or otherwise put down a learner's attempt or answer; eliminate the words "no" and "wrong" from their vocabularies; win the attention of learners away from preoccupations, distresses, and distractions; try to accept the expression of feelings, which if released appropriately in a safe setting can increase the learners' ability to learn; firmly interrupt put-downs and oppressive behavior to foster collective safety; use alternatives to grades in order to measure or recognize learning, like portfolios, demonstrations of knowledge, a capstone project.

YOUTHBUILD'S EDUCATION
SUCCESS AND CURRENT STATUS

Over the past five or six years, YouthBuild USA, through the its National Schools Initiative and Postsecondary Education Initiative, both funded in part by the Bill & Melinda Gates Foundation, has focused significant resources on developing diploma-granting and charter schools, deepening content and educational methodologies, and promoting access to and success in postsecondary education. As a result, as of 2013 there were 34 charter schools in a total of 55 Youth-Build programs that have a high school diploma as an option. Many YouthBuild programs are now directing their students to college and postsecondary training; 43 percent of students in the Postsecondary Education Initiative are enrolling in college; and 59 percent of college enrollees are continuing past the first critical year.

YouthBuild USA is increasingly part of the national conversation about educational reform and increasing the high school graduation rate. President Obama has challenged the nation to stem the drop-out rate and increase the high school graduation rate to 90 percent by 2020. YouthBuild is producing high school graduates from among the students who left traditional high schools without a diploma. A steadily rising percentage of YouthBuild's former high school drop-outs are now enrolling in college. Schools and education-policy makers are noticing our success. Some school districts are approaching local YouthBuild programs to become the official dropout recovery center for a school district, or to become a charter school, or to partner with community colleges to create a strong bridge to postsecondary learning, and so on.

Furthermore, three major national initiatives have agreed to focus on 6.7 million *opportunity youth*—young people who are not in school or working. They are called opportunity youth for two reasons. One is that they need an opportunity; two is that they represent an opportunity for the nation, if the nation would invest in their education and development. The White House Council for Community Solutions decided to focus on opportunity youth. GradNation, formed to coordinate the President's goal of increasing high school graduates to 90 percent by 2020, has included disconnected youth in its scope of work. The Opportunity Youth Network, sponsored by the Aspen Institute, is organizing a broad coalition on behalf of reconnecting one million young people to education and employment.

Given these good developments, and to ensure that our education work is aligned with our social change mission, it is useful to think about what is the goal of education in YouthBuild, how could it better serve the long-range goals of social change, and how do we get there?

EDUCATION FOR LEADERSHIP DEVELOPMENT

In the last chapter we listed the five key reasons why leadership development is important. To review quickly:

1. Leadership calls forth higher potential in young people.

2. Leadership skills are sought by employers and colleges.

3. Emphasis on leadership leads to higher program outcomes.

4. Young people in leadership roles bring greater visibility and support to the program.

5. YouthBuild develops resources for the community to help tackle the issues of the day.

In my vision of YouthBuild at its fullest, the development of young leaders is seen as the central goal of the program. Leadership development is two-pronged: leadership for self and family, including work life; and leadership for the program, community, and the planet.

Leadership for oneself and family means gaining the skills, behaviors, and attitudes that allow one to handle one's own life successfully; things like achieving basic reading and writing literacy, going to college or a postsecondary credentialing program, building a career with a sustainable income, taking care of one's family responsibilities, and being a productive person. The wider world usually calls this kind of development "life skills," but YouthBuild USA has found it useful to consider this part of leadership development. It is included in its definition of good leadership as "taking responsibility to make things go right for self, family, program, community, and the planet."

Currently, YouthBuild programs put most of their attention on the first prong of leadership development, which represents the construction training, high school equivalency or academic component, and counseling and social services work. This part of our work is absolutely necessary but in itself does not lead to developing leadership for the purposes of engaging in the community.

The second prong is *leadership for the community*. This would include studying people's history, using a popular-education approach that starts with the lives of students and builds out, teaching leadership skills and competencies, doing community service and learning, understanding oppression and cultural identity, learning basic economic analysis, learning community organizing skills, participating in leadership opportunities (serving on the policy committee, speaking to the media or at city hall, shadowing a community worker or public official, doing a leadership job in the class or on the worksite), and so on.

THE PLACE OF EDUCATION
IN THE DEVELOPMENT OF LEADERS

Education is a key method for developing leaders. Education is different from schooling, although we often equate the two. As Mark Twain said, "I never let my schooling get in the way of my education."

Schooling is typically what happens in classrooms with teachers. Sometimes it can be good education, but more often, in too many public schools, it is irrelevant, conventional, uncreative, or boring at best, and oppressive, hierarchical, insulting, and crushing to inner confidence at worst. This is mostly why young people drop out of school.

YouthBuild is an alternative educational environment. The classroom is part of it, but, at its best, the entire program is a learning environment—offering young people the feeling the safety of a positive program culture, building a house, doing community service projects, serving on the policy committee, having a mentor, interning for jobs, and so on.

YouthBuild USA has produced great handbooks and materials on YouthBuild education, including the most recent *Education at a Youth-Build Program*. Here, I want to emphasize a few ideas related to viewing our education work as leadership work.

EDUCATION FOR THE WORLD OF WORK

Our basic obligation is to better equip YouthBuild students with the ability to secure and hold a job for starters, on the way to building a career of meaningful work. From studies and from interviews with employers, we know the things required by the world of work: punctuality, reliability, a positive attitude, ability to get along with others, and ability to work cooperatively on a team. In other words, be on time, do what you say you will do, be a nice person, be a team player, and don't cause trouble. Basic reading and writing competency is a must. Today, so is basic computer literacy. Having a GED or diploma tells the employer some of these things, so such a credential is helpful. Basically, most employers want workers who are trainable, are reliable, don't miss days, do a decent day's work, relate well to a team or to customers, and have a positive attitude.

So on basic preparation for work, we know that YouthBuild should emphasize the following skills:

- Improving reading and writing skills

- Developing solid skills necessary for construction, health-care, or information-technology fields

- Gaining industry-recognized credentials

- Insisting on high standards of production and hard work

- Building self-esteem (confidence, belief in self, etc.)

- Building self-presentation skills (dress, eye contact, posture, hand-shake, manners, etc.)

- Developing computer literacy (word processing, data entry and management, Internet access, e-mail, social media)

- Practicing job-readiness skills (résumé writing, interviewing, how to be a good employee, do's and don'ts, etc.)

- Developing teamwork and relationship skills

These are not easy to accomplish. Many YouthBuild programs find they can barely cover them in the short time they have with the young people, let alone get the students competent, confident, and comfortable enough to take on the world of work. But there are several things that could speed the acquisition of this set of skills:

- **Create a staff team that shares a common vision and plan for teaching these skills.** This will require that the teachers, construction trainers, counselors, and job-placement, life-skills, and leadership-development staff teach these skills in mutually reinforcing, cooperative ways. It means that they decompartmentalize the program, especially taking down the walls between the classroom and the worksite. It means developing a project-based approach, with real integration of academics, vocational education, and construction training. This implies that the director has such a vision, hires and trains a staff who embrace this vision, and holds staff accountable for implementing an integrated approach. This harkens back to the chapter on core values and program culture.

- **Develop a clearly articulated, measurable set of competencies** for "Education for the World of Work," which the program staff systematically guide students through. The US Department of Labor "SCANS" document is a good beginning.

- **Find or develop effective approaches for teaching or learning basic literacy and numeracy.** Lots of learning venues are needed that include individualized modules, computer-aided instruction, one-on-one tutors, and small ability-grouping sessions to move people at their own rates and take maximum advantage of individual learning styles. It might mean using a well-developed methodology like Mockingbird Education, which has been successfully adopted by many YouthBuild programs. Ideally, from the beginning of the program the counselor takes the lead, reinforced by the rest of the education team, to work with students on their self-esteem issues; help them build or rebuild positive, life-enhancing belief systems; and do individual and group counseling to help heal emotional hurts that hold them back or keep them acting in negative, self-destructive ways. (More on this in the next chapter, on counseling.)

- **The program needs a computer-skills trainer for the young people.** This trainer could be a volunteer or paid staff, but it should be someone who regularly teaches students typing, word processing, and basic data-entry skills, as well as Internet and social-media tools. If the program itself does not have the equipment or the trained personnel, it can arrange for this with another community agency, community college, or library. However it does it, the program must make a commitment to having computer education as a part of its basic package.

EDUCATION FOR LEADERSHIP AND CIVIC ENGAGEMENT

The other part of my ideal YouthBuild education approach is education for leadership, civic engagement, and lifelong learning. As difficult as achieving the skills and attitudes needed for the world of work is, it is only a part of what is necessary. Education for the world of work is necessary for individual success but not sufficient for social transformation. That takes education for leadership. Elements of this education include political and economic analysis, community-organizing skills, and leadership skills. The challenge is to teach the *skills* required for mastery of the high school equivalency or diploma by using *content* that is relevant and empowering. The following are some suggestions.

- **Find or create a culturally relevant curriculum** (for high school equivalency or diploma programs). Use a project-based learning approach that begins with the content of the students' lives and interests, and draws out all the relevant academic skills. The curriculum would be mapped to the literacy and social studies parts of the GED or state exams, but the students would gain a real education about their communities, the histories of their peoples and cultures, the skills of being a leader, the history of large social-change movements, and the role of young people in those movements.

- **Offer young people a coherent guide to the political and economic landscape.** The conditions of poor communities are directly impacted by the global economy. Yet the people in these communities are awash in misinformation and propaganda, misled and confused, and thus are less equipped to know how to organize to change things. YouthBuild programs need a course in basic economics from alternative viewpoints. (United for a Fair Economy, the Center for

Popular Economics, and the New Economy Coalition, are just three organizations that put out good material that could be adapted to YouthBuild populations. They have curricula, trainings, and deep working knowledge of the issues that poor and working people face.) The YouthBuild Charter School of California has developed a social-justice–oriented curriculum called the *ACE Manual*, developed by YouthBuild teachers, that is well worth checking out.

- **Review the leadership curriculum outline that is included in the** *Youth Leadership Development Handbook* (p. 117), written by Dorothy Stoneman. This was the curriculum worked out by the Youth Action Program's leadership school. The curriculum is fairly comprehensive, running the gamut from study of big social change movements in this century, to theory and understanding of oppression, to methods of dealing with emotional hurts which interfere with one's leadership, to methods of community organizing.

- **Use** *Blueprint for Democracy,* an excellent basic civics curriculum developed by local and national YouthBuild staff, and used by many YouthBuild programs. This curriculum, in part, makes a strong case for the importance of voting and taking part in the electoral process as a means of affecting change. The decisions made by the town council, the state legislature, or Congress have direct impact on the lives of YouthBuild students and their communities. But the fact that the dots are rarely connected for young people, coupled with their own sense that voting makes little difference, often keeps them from voting. So candidates don't pay them much mind, therefore the voices of the young people are not heard, and their interests not represented on the councils of power.

- **Have students read and discuss the** *Declaration of Inter-Dependence,* created by the YouthBuild National Alumni Council and Young Leaders Council. It is a policy paper on six critical issues that affect the lives and communities of YouthBuild young people.

- **Explore the field of popular education.** There are a number of people in this country doing good work around popular education, such as the Paulo Freire-based method of using the life experience of learners and the conditions of their communities to teach literacy and political empowerment. There are many good online resources on this topic—Google "popular education" for starters.

The following two sidebars, repeated from an earlier chapter, list a few ways that leadership development can be integrated into the classroom setting. Your imagination can invent an infinite variety.

Leadership Development in **Classroom Structure**

Young people:

- Help decide classroom activities
- Are responsible for finishing and correcting their own work
- Have opportunities to work in teams
- Teach each other
- Rotate leadership jobs in the classroom
- Participate in evaluating teachers

Leadership Development in the **Classroom Content**

Young people:

- Research topics of community concern or current event
- Make presentations to the class or entire program on a community issue
- Participate in formal debate
- Write letters to editors or Congresspeople
- Visit and dialogue with public officials
- Use *Blueprint for Democracy*, a civic-engagement curriculum from YouthBuild USA
- Study the history and culture of the racial and ethnic groups that students belong to
- Study the movements of poor people fighting for equal opportunity
- Learn about the climate crisis and become green leaders

THE YOUTHBUILD PROGRAM
DIRECTOR'S ROLE IN EDUCATION

The proposal to orient YouthBuild education even more directly toward both the world of work and leadership development calls for a specific conception of the role of the program director or manager. The program director or manager needs to be primarily thinking like a visionary school leader who can hire and train staff to work together in a concerted effort to assist the students to achieve competency in work and leadership skills.

The program's counselor is not just counseling but is also helping to implement the entire educational approach and laying the foundation of social-emotional learning environment. The teacher is not just using the high school equivalency preparation guide but is also teaching the skills needed to pass the test by using the methods of popular education, similarly for teaching that leads to a high school diploma. The construction trainer is not just teaching construction skills but is also setting up the site to promote leadership skills. The job developer is not just finding job possibilities in isolation from the counselors or teachers but is also using the job-readiness classes and interviews as leadership opportunities.

And so on. The program director or manager needs to coordinate all this, while also setting up systems of communication, record keeping, and staff interaction that dovetail toward the desired objectives. The program director will be hiring people in every one of these positions who are "teachers," in the best sense of that word. Ideally, the program director or manager will also have deep experience with creative forms of education. Where this is not the case, the director would engage progressive and successful visionary education leaders as advisors.

THE TEACHERS

Of course, the teacher makes or breaks a classroom. From everything that has been said about YouthBuild as primarily a leadership-development program, it should be obvious that the YouthBuild teacher is not a typical public high school teacher. Throughout the YouthBuild network there are very many gifted, creative, and effective teachers. To the extent possible, I would hire someone as a teacher who embodied the following combination of skills, qualities, and attitudes:

- Knows how to care and show the love and respect needed to get students beyond the huge load of frustration, fear, and failure that they carry from their prior school experiences

- Already practices the core values of the program

- Sees the entire YouthBuild program as a learning environment, and can build a classroom culture of respect that mirrors the larger program culture

- Understands why youth leadership development is job number one, and will orient the curriculum towards leadership for self and the community

- Knows that everything speaks, and sets his or her classroom up to speak leadership

- Is a leader in his or her own life, and is actively engaged in the wider world

- Understands the role of teaching as essentially facilitating learning, rather than lecturing or embracing a teacher-centered approach

- Has deep experience using project-based learning, popular-education approach, critical-thinking methods, and creative-learning techniques

- Has a track record of creating a cooperative, harmonious, high quality student-centered learning environment with high expectations, and is experienced in both individual and group learning

- Has a well-developed understanding of the world systems and can help students connect the dots among things like the global economy, poverty and wealth, the shape of the environment, conditions in low-income communities, and so on; and can help young people shape a vision of a caring and sustainable world and strategies for getting there

- Can move students through the necessary achievement benchmarks like the high school equivalency or diploma by using high-quality educational methods and content, without focusing primarily on testing

- Really enjoys young people!

You might think that this describes superman or superwoman, that it's impossible to find someone with all this. It is admittedly daunting, and all this may not come in one person. But it is easier to build toward this to the extent that the YouthBuild director and current staff share a commitment to leadership development, high-quality education that supports leadership development, and a clear vision for what the classroom learning environment should look and feel like. Then either the current teacher(s) can move in this direction through training and support, or your next teacher candidate search is more clearly defined.

THE STUDENTS

The core constituents in YouthBuild are the students. To be true to the mission of leadership development and to developing relevant, high-quality education, the core constituents must be involved in decisions about their education. We are determined not to re-create some of the worst elements of the oppressive, disrespectful, and discriminatory school institutions that drove YouthBuild young people out in the first place.

Therefore, setting aside learning content for this section, there are several structural features that need to be part of a holistic YouthBuild education model:

- **Students involved in teacher selection.** Students would be involved in interviewing and selecting teachers. As part of the process, a teacher candidate would have to teach at least one complete class to students, who would give their assessment of the teacher. The policy committee would normally participate in candidate interviews and selection, but it could ask more students to provide input and assessment. As with all hiring, this is a cooperative power-sharing process between the students and the director and staff. Consensus is needed, not rigid majority rule or director decision. If the director hired a teacher that the students did not support, that teacher would face student resistance at best, or deliberate undermining at worst, and the director would lose credibility in the eyes of the students. On the other hand, if the director agreed to hire someone the students like but that he or she doesn't think is qualified or suited for the position, this is an abdication of the director's leadership responsibility. Both director and young people on the policy committee have to agree. This insures a better selection, supported by all. Directors should not refer to the policy committee for interviewing anyone that they would not be comfortable hiring.

- **Students involved in designing the classroom.** In cooperation with the teacher near the beginning of the year, but after students have bought into YouthBuild, the young people would be invited to redesign the look and feel of the classroom(s) that worked for both them and the teacher. Through the arrangement of furniture, colors, images, lighting, and so on, they help make it their own space, reflecting their interests, cultures, creativity, and aspirations. Remember, everything speaks!

- **Students involved in determining pieces of the curriculum.** Along popular-education lines, as much as possible, draw learning pieces out from the lives and concerns of the students, making curriculum relevant and interesting. (Again, Google "popular education" for ideas.) I am not saying that all learning starts and ends with a student's life, only that a student's life should be honored and mined for its richness.

- **Students involved in evaluation of teachers.** If all schools sought input from students on the character, quality, and skill of teachers, this alone would move school improvement miles down the road. In YouthBuild we want to walk this talk, asking students to assess the teachers on a regular basis. This makes student voice real and makes teachers accountable to their main audience. This evaluation could be done by anonymous surveys developed by the policy council, or existing surveys from organizations that have developed evaluation tools could be used.

- **Students teach and lead in learning.** In the spirit of building a cooperative, inclusive, intentional learning environment, students would teach what they know, tutor other students, create a supportive peer-learning atmosphere, be appreciated for their unique gifts and talents, and rotate leadership roles in the classroom.

EDUCATION IS KEY TO LIBERATION

My hope is that ideas for YouthBuild education sketched in this chapter appeal to you. It's not that these ideas are necessarily new. Many YouthBuild programs are already doing some of them. What might be new is consciously positioning the education work as serving YouthBuild's North Star—integrating education for success in college and the world of work with education for leadership and critical consciousness. Education is key to transformation, both of individual young people and of our society. Thus YouthBuild's approach to education and learning needs to be ambitious. It should be debated and thought about deeply and widely. All our assumptions and practices about education bear examining in light of our core values and long-range mission. Our educational practice and culture should promote love, learning, leadership, and liberation. YouthBuild teachers, directors, staff, current students, graduates, and YouthBuild USA and supporters all have a huge stake in shape and future of YouthBuild education.

8

Counseling and Healing

"Never before have I ever been in an environment where
I've been appreciated for just being who I am; very honest,
determined, caring, and understanding…YouthBuild
has taught me that it's OK to be yourself."

TaRhea Ray, from a YouthBuild program in Los Angeles

"When I leave YouthBuild at the end of the day, I can't wait to get
back the next day. At home I lie in bed thinking about the fact that I
am building a house for a homeless mother and child…I used to think
I was a bad person. Staff helped me find my real self. Now I just want
to belong to a great movement to bring respect to my peers."

James Gates, YouthBuild St. Louis graduate

T his chapter is a strong call to deepen the practice of counseling, in order to speed the process of healing, in order to
round out the development of young leaders. Counseling and
healing are complex and involved processes. There are excellent handbooks and resources that cover a multitude of aspects of this topic for
YouthBuild programs (see the many resources listed at the back of this
book, especially the *Counseling and Case Management at a YouthBuild*

Program). There is also a wealth of knowledge and best practices among the many YouthBuild counselors in the field. It is not my intent in this chapter to replicate these resources. I want to offer a few reflections on the current practice and to point to some improvements that are implied by the focus on YouthBuild as the training ground for young leaders.

YouthBuild young people started out life with enormous intelligence, endless curiosity, natural desire to cooperate, a deep capacity for love and attachment, infinite creativity, innate joy, and an inborn capacity for learning and caring. They have tremendous talents and gifts, have shown courage and resilience in handling their lives, even while sometimes making mistakes. But by the time they get to YouthBuild, they have been pretty beat up by life—by racism, poverty, abuse, oppression, poor education, violence, family trauma, broken communities, broken homes, broken promises, broken hearts. They show up with any number of bad habits and bad feelings about themselves and others.

So part of the purpose of YouthBuild is to help young people recover as much of their inherent nature as possible. This is deep and important work. To do this a program has to provide young people with a safe environment, emotionally and physically. It needs to provide caring and skilled adults who can balance kindness and acceptance with accountability and discipline. It needs to have staff who are trained and effective in what they do, and who understand that their real work is human transformation. The program needs to be long enough to allow young people to solidify the gains made, with plenty of ways for them to plug in. The program needs to be comprehensive enough to provide young people with most of what they need for development: a healthy environment, positive role models, a positive peer culture, a quality learning situation, real skill development that prepares them for work, a little money coming in, patience with their bad patterns, and love and acceptance. To the extent that these conditions are present, then young people are able to rebuild their lives.

COUNSELING AND PERSONAL CHANGE IN A YOUTHBUILD CONTEXT

YouthBuild young people typically have several kinds of issues that they need help with, as listed and explained below.

Crises
First are the crises that fall into their lives during the program cycle—things like a health issue, a pregnancy, a domestic-abuse situation, the death of a family member, or an arrest for alleged criminal activity.

Life skills
Second are the life-skills needs—things like learning how to parent, eat nutritious food, live within a budget, keep a schedule, practice personal hygiene, overcome an addiction, create a résumé, develop good work habits, and so on.

Deep developmental needs or trauma
The third encompasses the deeper developmental issues like the need for developing basic trust, loving oneself, opening up one's compassion, eliminating the effects of internalized oppression and powerlessness, recovering from early trauma or abuse, feeling connected to people, or having optimism and confidence about the future.

Issues Youth Bring to Program

- Physical violence or sexual abuse
- Loss of, abandonment by, or absence of one or more parents
- Substance abuse
- Discrimination and oppression
- Health issues
- Homelessness
- Learning disabilities
- Criminal or gang activity
- Troubled romantic relationships
- Low self-esteem, self-love, self-confidence
- Lack of trust
- Lack of positive values or role models
- Fear of success or failure
- More

The deep hurts at this third level actually predispose young people to more crises and greater life-skill needs because life has not gone well for them, and early hurts often leave them less equipped emotionally to handle the inevitable challenges of living. So strategically, if YouthBuild were to provide maximum assistance to young people to turn their lives around, staff and counselors would focus mostly on the early developmental issues. Certainly YouthBuild programs are committed to the personal development and transformation of young people. However, the results are often less than desired due to various reasons:

- Typically staff and counselors spend most of their time helping students handle their crises, putting out fires, and teaching life skills, and rarely get to the deeper developmental issues. Crises demand attention; help is needed in the moment or else something worse might happen. Staff also know that teaching young people to navigate in the world requires them to develop adequate life skills.

- A program might lack sufficient funds to hire the right counselor to do the deeper personal change work. This work requires a counselor who is not only trained but knows how to create safety and trust, is a superb listener, can welcome the strong emotions of the young people, and is able to be a steady guide to young people in their efforts to heal their hardest emotional pain.

- A program director might not have had enough of an orientation to emotional healing to provide a vision for this work or know what kind of counselor to hire.

- A program might not know how to implement an integrated approach to counseling and personal development. The staff might have insufficient staff training to know how to build a cohesive program culture that supports it. Other real program demands or deliverables might squeeze out much attention from counseling and personal growth.

A strong counseling approach provides an opportunity to weave together the hard- and soft-skill areas of growth across other components. This work is based on a fundamental premise: any long-lasting change involves both outward behavior change and inner personal change. One without the other is not enough. Certifications, job training, high school equivalency or diploma, and hard skills are absolutely critical to graduate success. And so is personal development, the so-called soft skills. I once heard a CEO of a big company say that "we hire for hard skills but we fire for soft skills." The emotional and mental health issues of young people impact all the areas of life that they want to succeed in: gaining confidence and self-respect, learning and advancing one's education; developing good work habits and sustaining meaningful employment, nurturing one's family and healthy relationships, caring for one's body and health, contributing to the program and the community, navigating a diverse world, making something of oneself, and living a positive lifestyle.

COUNSELING AND HEALING ARE DIFFERENT

Counseling

It might be helpful to draw a distinction between *counseling*, which is what the counselor does, and *healing*, which is what the young person does. The counselor can facilitate the process of healing. The counselor's role, indeed the role of the whole program, is to assist young people to know themselves, understand their impact and relationships to others, and to navigate the wider world. The counselor has lots of tools.

- *For understanding the self,* the counselor can hold one-on-one counseling sessions; listen deeply; ask questions like "Who Am I?"; teach peer counseling; help students acknowledge their gifts and talents; use a steady dose of validation and appreciation; help students examine their mistaken assumptions and ineffective behavior; be a cheerleader, coach, advocate, mentor, support, and advisor. Young people come with deep emotional scars. Recovering from this level of hurt is take enormous safety and hard work, and young people will need the encouragement and guidance of a skilled counselor (and a positive peer culture) to keep at it.

- *For understanding relationships with others,* a key methodology is counseling groups in which one's behavior is reflected back by members of the group. Also helpful are equal-time support groups, 12-step groups, separate women's groups and men's groups (often called "sister-to-sister" and "brother-to-brother" in YouthBuild). The more general approach is to establish a positive, healthy program culture overall, in which peers appreciate one another and hold each other accountable.

- *For understanding how to navigate the wider world,* life skills are the main teaching mode. This is also the domain of the "case management" part of counseling—having a wide network of referral agencies to help handle the crises and life needs of students. Leadership development and preparation for the world of work, described in earlier chapters, are part of this process.

Healing

However, it is only the young person who does the healing, and recovering from early hurts will take much longer than the span of a YouthBuild program cycle. So it is even more important that students learn ways of helping themselves and each other, tools they can use all their lives that are not dependent on a counselor or a program. Thus, in my ideal YouthBuild program, the counselor would introduce students to a range of self-help tools. This would include teaching a theory or theories of human nature and emotional health, and reasons for dysfunction that can provide a rough map of human development. Different YouthBuild programs have effectively taught and utilized the following methods, the details of which can easily be found through an online search for words and phrases such as peer counseling, journaling, poetry, rhyming, meditation and yoga, self-appreciation, stress management, restorative practices, nonviolent communication (NVC), TruThought®, Power Source®, and circle process.

TOOLS FOR TRANSFORMATION

I would like to sketch out a proposal for how a program might systematically offer young people such lifelong tools for their own healing and development that, once learned and practiced, are not dependent on a counselor or program.

Assumptions

The proposal below rests on several assumptions:

- Young people are at different stages of personal development. Therefore, an effective counseling approach needs to provide exposure to different kinds of tools. One size does not fit all.

- It is possible within the timeframe of a yearlong YouthBuild program and a coordinated approach for young people to learn specific new skills, attitudes, beliefs, and habits that can significantly help them handle their lives more effectively.

- Such tools would reduce personal backsliding among graduates; it would also help maintain higher attendance and retention while in the program.

- In addition to the skills and caring that YouthBuild counselors bring, we need to look beyond YouthBuild for well-developed expertise in the area of human transformation.

- Effective counselors or resources come in all flavors, both the same as and different from the cultural backgrounds of the YouthBuild students. Powerful lessons and tools can be learned from people very different from oneself.

- There are many organizations and expert practitioners who would be eager to work with local YouthBuild programs. YouthBuild staff and young people deserve to be exposed to the state-of-the-art in the human change technologies available.

- Staff as well as young people need these tools, both for their own mental health and to develop their capacity and skill level to do this work with young people. Therefore, the model below includes staff as learners.

- The proposal to deepen our approach to counseling is not more important than nor intended to override the other crucial areas which call to be sustained or improved. It is a next step in the development of YouthBuild.

- Finally, this approach does not substitute for the crucial role of a program counselor who cares, is there every day, and assists young people with many aspects of life. Hopefully, the counselor, the young people, and the program will be deepened by the cumulative outside resources proposed below.

Proposal

Define and secure resource people for a series of six to eight weekly classes to be offered during the YouthBuild program cycle. Each class would include both young people and staff in workable numbers. Each class cycle would feature a specific approach to personal change and be taught or facilitated by an experienced practitioner of that approach. Each cycle would include both theory and practice, and be followed by a retreat into that methodology to solidify the skills learned. The assumptions are that not one size fits all; that different methods will work for different people at different stages of growth; and that including staff will help build local capacity. Participants would evaluate the effectiveness of each approach and recommend changes or adaptations. Below is a sampling of possible six-to-eight-week class cycles, some of which local YouthBuild programs have already implemented.

- **Stress reduction.** A well-developed field with many practical applications and local practitioners. Includes recognizing sources and symptoms of stress, managing stress, short-term stress-busting techniques, and life-changing stress-reduction methods.

- **Conflict resolution and anger management.** Includes building listening and communication skills, learning to give constructive feedback and de-escalate conflict. There are skilled practitioners in most localities.

- **Healthy relationships.** For several years, about 20 YouthBuild programs, initially trained by YouthBuild USA, have been implementing a course called "Love Notes." Staff and students alike testify to its effectiveness. There are many other resources for this critical area of a young person's life.

- **Re-evaluation Counseling.** The theory and practice of peer counseling. Includes a theory of human nature and human change, a practical set of skills for being a peer counselor, and effective methods for creating safe conditions for emotional release. Certified instructors all over the country. (This is the method that Dorothy and I have used for the past 40 years to handle our stress, heal old wounds, and to recover from inevitable disappointments and heart-breaks in YouthBuild and life.)

- **Meditation and yoga.** Includes mindfulness meditations noting thoughts and feelings, guided visualizations, music meditation, body scan and progressive relaxation, and yoga postures. Practitioners throughout the country.

- **Landmark Forum.** A spin-off of EST (Erhard Seminar Training). Emphasizes personal responsibility, no excuses, personal power and possibility, and successful goal setting. Powerful group experiences. Instructors in many locations throughout the country.

- **Process Psychology.** A method of group exploration of roles and issues, based on the work of Arnold Mindell. Includes role plays and role reversals, dramatization of unspoken thoughts and feelings. A skilled group of practitioners in many parts of the country.

- **High-performance methodology.** Incorporates many aspects of self-affirmation, visualization of success, diet for maximum energy, development of empowering beliefs. Utilized in business and athletics. Practitioners are available locally.

- **Nutrition and wellness.** Guidelines for personal health including nutrition information, developing a good diet and eating habits, developing empowering concepts of one's health and body, practicing an exercise routine, massage and body care. Practitioners are in every part of the country.

- **Choice Theory.** Derived from the work of William Glasser PhD. Emphasizes behavior change, personal responsibility and consequences, and taking complete charge of oneself.

- **Rites of passage.** Some programs use beautiful ceremonies to mark a stage of development or a milestone of achievement.

- **Restorative justice.** Methods of handling discipline and restoring relationships based on mutual dialogue and understanding that is an alternative to punishment.

- **And many others** to choose from.

These classes would be mainly experiential. Participants would practice the methods and skills offered, certainly in the class itself, and hopefully beyond. Obviously, this would take commitment, resources, scheduling, and coordination. YouthBuild staff would need to be part of the classes, both for their own learning and to be able to provide some follow-up. Outside teachers would need to be screened or coached on working with YouthBuild students. Their materials or methods would need to be culturally relevant and accessible. But exposing students to a variety of human-transformation skills that they may not have access to otherwise can be a huge benefit to individuals and to the program. I urge programs to experiment with this proposal.

STAFF ROLES IN COUNSELING

It is obvious that the kind of personal change that we have been talking about does not just happen in the program's counseling component or just with the counselor. The counselor has a leadership role, but the entire staff is involved in creating the environment that fosters personal growth. Here are a few reminders on this point:

- The program director needs to put forth to the staff a vision of YouthBuild as a leadership-development and transformational process so that they understand their roles in this effort.

- In addition to expected qualifications, the counselor, as mentioned above, needs to be able and willing to welcome the emotions of young people as part of their healing process.

- The rest of the staff need to be trained in the three goals of the counseling process (to help young people understand themselves, understand their impact and relationships with others, and effectively navigate the systems of the wider world), and know their roles in implementing them.

These three goals need to be integrated across program components and built into the culture. For example: staff are trained in effective listening; life skills are taught by many staff, both formally and informally; the leadership competencies (see page 110) are taught by various staff across the program; listening circles and support groups happen in many corners of the program; the practice of appreciations and shout-outs happen everywhere regularly; staff become skilled in cultural competence and help with issues of diversity; goal setting is implemented across components; practices for body, mind, heart, and spirit are a program norm; a language of mutual respect is expected; young people are involved in decision making throughout the program; the counselor regularly spends time on the worksite and in the classroom; the job placement person works hand-in-hand with the counselor on student job preparation.

Programwide Context That Supports Counseling, Healing, and Transformation

- Program philosophy or method
- A thorough youth orientation
- A contract and infraction system; consistent discipline
- A pledge recited by the group that internalizes values
- Rituals, recognition, and rites of passage
- Social, cultural, and community-building activities
- Youth participation in decision making
- Leadership-development opportunities
- Thoroughgoing mutual respect

RECOMMENDED SELF-DEVELOPMENT PRACTICES

In the next sections, I want to highlight five areas of self-development practice that I recommend highly:

1. Body, mind, heart, and spirit practices for young people
2. Equal-time support groups
3. Exploration of issues of oppression and diversity
4. A positive approach to substance abuse
5. The systematic use of appreciation

I recommend these because they are tools and processes that young people can use all their lives for their own healing and self development.

One thing that a counselor can do is to help each young person create a set of personal practices that help him or her move toward the goals, practices that can be used well beyond the life of the program. All YouthBuild programs ask young people to set short and long term goals in the context of creaing what we have called a "life plan." In my experience, goals need consistent practices that provide the scaffolding, so to speak, for building success. The following model is along those lines.

Recommended self-development practice 1

Body, mind, heart, and spirit practices for young people

Much of our behavior is determined by the condition of our body, mind, heart, and spirit. If we take good care of these four key areas of our life, then our behavior, which includes our words and actions, our habits and goals, our successes and achievements, will naturally be healthier and more effective. Or, from the other direction, we set goals that will require us to develop our bodies, our minds, our hearts, or our spirits in various ways in order to achieve those goals.

There are many paths to self-improvement, and no single path will fit everyone. But once a young person decides to change, or to improve his or her life, or to pursue a long-range goal of success, or to live a quality life, then there are many ways to go about it.

So what would young people need or want or use as elements of a holistic practice of change? First, there has to be alignment between what a person wants as a goal and the means or practice for getting there. Can we create a holistic practice aimed at keeping a balance in the development of one's body, mind, heart, and spirit? Can we get skilled in asking a young person about his or her goals, then helping to design a balanced practice aimed at achieving those goals?

For example, let's say a young person sets a long-range goal of graduating from college. To succeed, he or she would have to keep cultivating the belief that success is possible, and counter likely feelings that try to make him or her give up. He or she will have to research the right college or university setting, figure out how to pay for it, learn how to manage time, learn how to study independently, make new friends among peers and teachers, deal with many obstacles and setbacks, and take care of his or her body and health to maintain the energy and stamina to study hard.

Some young people may not have a specific goal, but want to get their life together or start living a positive lifestyle. At any time, a young person can define a program of self-improvement in four areas of human life—body, mind, heart, and spirit. To start simply, he or she might try attending to just one item in each of the areas to get used to a disciplined practice. More or different elements can be added over time, depending on the individual's goals and stage of development. Below is a sample menu of practices to be shared with students, each of which has many steps, as detailed below.

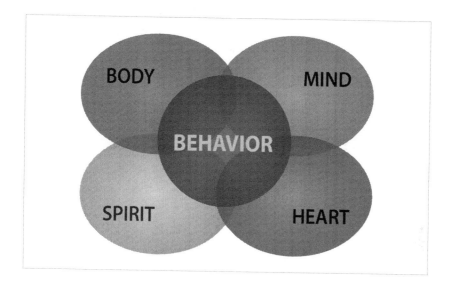

Body

- Promote physical safety: Don't carry weapons; stay away from dangerous areas and situations.

- Learn about nutrition and practice a healthy diet; lose weight if overweight.

- Exercise regularly, including muscle strengthening, stretching, and aerobics.

- Get enough restful sleep to renew your energy and stamina.

- Learn what toxic substances do to the body; decrease intake of toxins.

- Create affirmations about the body; repeat daily.

Mind

- Unearth limiting beliefs about yourself and formulate the opposite; use this as an affirmation.

- Know that people get smarter and smarter the more they learn.

- Learn the basics of reading, writing, math, and communicating effectively.

- Appreciate your own intelligence all the time; even making mistakes is a miracle!

- Learn to cultivate positive beliefs while also having healthy skepticism.

- Define a course of study and pursue it diligently; get help when stuck.

- Attain your high school equivalency or diploma.

- Pursue higher education: community college, trade school, university, or apprenticeship.

- Notice the effects of your thoughts, words, and deeds on yourself and others; decide to practice building up rather than tearing down with your thoughts, words, and deeds.

- Safeguard your mind and heart from sources of upset: certain movies, videos, conversations, people, news, substances, and so on.

Heart

- Appreciate yourself in as many ways as possible, all the time.

- Get help with emotional problems and old hurts so they don't interfere with your goals.

- Develop a deep trust with someone with whom you can open your heart—a safe person with whom you can let yourself cry, feel scared, let out your anger without hurting others.

- Notice what makes you happy and take yourself there whenever needed. Examples: listening to positive music, being with a special person, taking a walk in a beautiful place, reading inspiring things, meditating or praying, and so on.

- Hold an image of yourself that is in the direction of your greatest potential.

- Decide to practice kindness, generosity, and compassion, even when you may feel angry or vengeful; notice the impact on yourself and others when you do this.

Spirit

- Cultivate a prayer or meditation practice.

- Find spiritually inspiring things; dip into them regularly.

- Explore your culture's spiritual roots or traditions.

- View yourself as a sacred being: inherently valuable, worthy of respect.

Recommended self-development practice 2

Equal-time support groups

There is much personal support that happens informally in most groups. However, having a formal support group is very helpful. The basic idea is for people to gather together as a regular group simply to listen to how it has been for each other on a feeling level. Small groups of four to eight are best, since this size allows more time for each individual. If your group is larger than eight, divide it into smaller groups. Protect the time by asking people to turn off their phones, by allotting enough time (one hour minimum), and by meeting in as pleasant a place as possible.

Support groups can provide safe spaces for people to vent, or deal with an emotional issue that has been troubling them, or feel cared about by others. There are many kinds of support groups. The following are some that have been used successfully in YouthBuild programs.

- **Support groups for people with similar backgrounds.** YouthBuild programs have formed regular support groups for women, men, parents, people on parole, recovering addicts, and so on. The safety of being with people with similar experiences often allows people to open up more easily, since they don't have to explain certain things.

- **Rap groups** (called by different names like "keep-it-real" groups, or "brother-to-brother" or "sister-to-sister" groups, and so on) are commonly used in programs for youth and young adults. In these groups, the young people are free to bring up whatever is on their minds. Sometimes the counselor or facilitator opens up the topic. Topics have included many important subjects like family, spirituality, how to deal with violence, overcoming addiction, male and female relationships, racism, fear of failing, fear of succeeding.

- **Informal support groups.** Support groups can happen anywhere. Some YouthBuild construction crews meet on the construction site at the end of a workweek to review. Each person is given a turn while the others listen. It is a kind of support group. Sometimes the construction trainer asks the young people to talk about questions such as: *What have I accomplished or done well this week? What did I learn on the site this week? How was I a leader on the job this week? How could we be an even better team?*

Equal-time support groups of four-to-six people

Each of the types of groups listed above has its uses. However, I have found that equal-time support groups have the most universal use and are fairly easy to teach and learn. Basically, these are structured so that each person gets equal time to talk while the others give the speaker respectful, undivided attention. People can either talk about whatever they individually choose, or the group can choose a topic. But taking equal turns and really listening to each other is the key process. Knowing they will get a turn lets people relax and pay better attention. Begin with each person in turn sharing something that is going well for him, either personally or in his work. The purpose of this is to remind ourselves of the positive aspects of our lives, despite how we may be feeling at any one moment. Beginning this way usually raises the tone of the group, provides chances to celebrate each other's good news, and draws our attention away from what might be upsetting.

Then divide the remaining time equally among those present, each taking a turn to be listened to by the others who pay attention actively, looking at the speaker with warmth, caring, and no judgment. This is the heart of the process: learning how to listen to one another in such a way that people feel encouraged to share what is troubling them. Each of us is eager for someone to really listen and be interested. It seems that in day-to-day life, each of us is continually checking out the people we are with in a computer-like calculation, assessing how safe it is to share what is going on with us. When people are listened to with respect, warmth, and lack of judgment, they spontaneously begin to bring up what they need to talk about at the moment. Using the equal-time sharing format, each person gets an uninterrupted turn of equal length to simply say what's on his or her mind. After their time speaking, the people on either side of them appreciate them simply by telling them what they like about them.

Releasing feelings

As trust develops in the group, individual members may deepen their emotional sharing with a natural releasing of feelings: tears, fears, laughter, anger. This is healing. We humans have a built-in drive to heal ourselves of hurts. This can be seen most clearly in young children. What do they do when they get hurt? Cry. This is natural. They try to get someone's attention to the hurt so they can heal from it immediately. No one has to teach them to cry. They have to be taught to stop crying. And that is exactly what happened to most of us while growing up. Our natural healing process got tampered with by older people around us who told us, in one way or another, not to cry, or laugh too loudly, or be scared, or get mad. The result: each of us is carrying unhealed hurts from the past which infect our daily lives.

Given enough safety, encouragement, and time, we are eager to tell someone how it really is, and was, for us. If someone listens to us attentively and warmly, over time we will cry about the losses, disappointments, and endings in our lives; feel scared about things we couldn't admit before; laugh at the embarrassments; and feel the flashing rise of anger and rage about injustice we have witnessed.

Whenever we listen to people's life stories, we are usually inspired by the heroism in their lives, and how well they have survived, given everything that has come down on them. We gain respect for how well they are functioning, despite emotional distresses. Intuitively, we know that we ourselves would be better off if we lightened that load of distress.

The short-term effect of releasing feelings in these ways is that we clear our heads somewhat and function better. Having a good cry about a problem will not make the problem go away. But a good cry usually enhances our ability to deal with the problem. The long-range effect is that we begin to recover from the difficult experiences that made us feel insecure or unloved, or made us act timidly or over aggressively, or got in the way of intimate relationships, or made us think we were stupid, selfish, and incompetent, or any of a host of other ways our human functioning was interfered with by the hurtful experiences that came our way.

Never push for emotional release

While the expression of feelings is likely to occur spontaneously if the group is sufficiently attentive and caring, the facilitator should never urge or push for emotional release. This will be seen or felt as manipulative. Since feelings are scary, any urgency or eagerness about the importance of expressing them is unnerving. The adult just needs to be comfortable with them if they do come up.

If tears should start to flow, a simple comment like *It's OK to cry, go right ahead. It's good to get it out.* will help. On the other hand, angry feelings that are being dumped on another person in an insulting or hurtful way should be interrupted, or the security of the group will be lost. The support group will have an important positive effect if open and honest talking is taking place. The deeper healing of emotional release may or may not take place, depending on the circumstances. The adult needs to be sensitive to people's fears.

Concepts and guidelines for equal-time support groups

The following concepts and guidelines help emotional support to flourish:

- Feelings are just feelings. They can be felt, but they don't necessarily need to be acted upon. The more intense the feeling, the less likely it is to be a useful guide to action. Intense feelings often cloud our thinking. We can just let the feelings be shared and released, so they don't continue to distort the way we see reality. Simply accept the feelings, occasionally reminding people that they do not need to act on the feelings, just dump them out, and later they'll be able to figure things out better.

- Avoid giving advice or even telling similar experiences. People need our attention so they can release the distress feelings that interfere with their own thinking.

- Maintain strict confidentiality. That is, do not tell anyone outside the group what the person shared, and do not bring it up again to the person, unless he or she initiates the discussion.

- Remember to distinguish people from their feelings. People can temporarily have very bad feelings. They need others to know that these are not permanent and not who they are. It is most helpful to view the people always as wholesome, creative, essentially loving, very smart, and capable. And whenever they are not like this, some stress, old or new, has made them act differently.

- It is never useful to dump angry feelings on someone in an insulting way in the name of honesty.

- Equal-time sharing meetings work best when there is a skilled person in charge to set the tone, see that the time limits are kept, remind people how to listen, if necessary, and think about how the whole group is functioning.

- It is good to close the sharing with some form of appreciations of each other. This can take different forms. For example, the person on either side of the speaker can each tell the speaker something they like or admire about the speaker, or each person in turn can appreciate the person on the left (or right). See the last section in this chapter for more variations.

One last point. Even though an equal-time support group can be done without any adults or staff, it is best if a staff person teaches the process first until the young people can hold the format themselves. For a brief introduction to the theory and practice in YouthBuild, see my article "A Process of Emotional Healing."

HOW TO LEAD A SUPPORT GROUP

Step 1. Set a warm and friendly tone at the beginning and get the people to sit in a close circle. Four to six people per group.

Step 2. Remind people to practice the Attitudes of Good Listening:
- Approval and respect
- Warm attention to each speaker
- Eye contact
- No judgment
- No advice
- Acceptance of feelings
- Safety
- Confidentiality
- Appreciation
- Physical reassurance, as appropriate

Step 3. Ask each person to briefly say what is going well for them or share some good news they have (approximately one minute per person).

Step 4. Divide the remaining time (minus 10 minutes for appreciations, below) equally among the members of the group.

Step 5. Each person then gets a chance to speak without interruption for the allotted time with the full attention of the group. Have someone keep time.

Step 6. After each person speaks, the people sitting on either side appreciate one or two things about that person. Then move on to the next person, and so on.

Step 7. At the end, thank people for giving good attention to each other. Initiate a group hug or group appreciation if it seems appropriate.

Notes: Support groups work best with four to six people, so each person gets a decent amount of time. People can use their turn to talk about anything they want. If it is the group's first meeting, it is a good idea to suggest that people tell their life stories. It helps if the time keeper gives the speaker a 30-second warning before the time is up. Pass the watch each turn. If someone gets emotional, welcome the feelings; consider moving closer or holding them if it seems right. Don't get worried. People have a lot of feelings waiting for a chance to be heard. Often these feelings come out easier and sooner than the young people or you might expect. The quality of attention to each person is what makes this work. Encourage people to give their very best attention.

Recommended self-development practice 3

Exploration of issues of oppression and diversity

Oppression has taken an enormous toll on the lives of YouthBuild young people. The daily insults and institutional barriers they've experienced have created deep wounds and serious inhibitions on their lives, their communities, and their leadership. Since YouthBuild is intent on promoting their leadership, the programs need to become even more skilled at dealing with these issues.

In 1992, an African American director of a YouthBuild program said to me that if we were not deliberately helping young people in our programs deal with the effects of racism on their lives, then we were wasting their time. (He actually expressed it more colorfully!) As we thought about what this would mean in a program setting, I found myself expanding this challenge into a four-part framework for doing the personal change work around all oppressions. Originally meant to apply to work with young people in youth programs, it fits many groups and levels in society. The version here is a generalized framework.

In short, the framework says that in order to deal with oppression in a holistic way, people need ways to *inform* themselves about diversity issues, *heal* from the emotional hurts due to oppression, learn effective ways to *cope* with the ongoing daily oppression, and to *get involved in the efforts to eliminate* all forms of oppression and injustice.

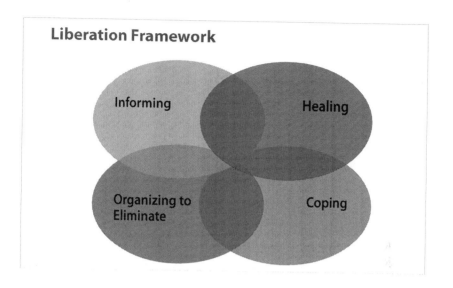

Liberation Framework

- Informing
- Healing
- Organizing to Eliminate
- Coping

INFORMING. Helping people create a coherent analysis of oppression. There is much truth in the old adage that knowledge is power. Knowledge helps us understand ourselves and others, and navigate the world. From a certain perspective, the history of the world has been shaped by the mistreatment and disrespect of one group after another: by tyranny, slavery, oppression, injustice, and cruelty; by humans hurting other humans causing untold suffering. Arguably, most of the ways people feel bad about themselves come from having been raised in a particular group, gender, race, religion, or nationality. It helps to develop a clear understanding of what oppression is *as a whole system*—the ideology, the structural and institutional components, the interpersonal dynamics, the internalization. (See my article "Four Is of Oppression" for an explanation of this system.) An analysis should also break down in simple, graspable terms, how different oppressions are related to each other, and what, if any, are the common roots. It would also include some of the history and facts around oppression and sketch out the key elements of a process of liberation from oppression.

HEALING. *Helping to heal from the emotional hurts of oppression.* Such knowledge can be helpful, but no matter how much information we have, most of us are walking around with huge loads of emotional hurt due to oppression. This weighs heavily on us; we have to learn, grow, and sometimes just survive while carrying this load. The pain sometimes boils over in rage; sometimes it stifles us in depression or hopelessness. It makes us less effective in life than we would be otherwise. So in our work with ourselves and other people, we need to learn how to provide times and spaces to release some of that pain. We need to create enough safety to share on the feeling level.

COPING. *Helping to develop effective ways of coping with oppression.* No matter how well we are informed or how much healing we have done, oppression is waiting for us just around the corner, every day, in real-life terms. We live and work in an oppressive society. There are many ways a program can help young people deal more effectively with oppression. For example: learning to handle sexually harassing behavior, studying one's legal rights in cases of discrimination, learning to act or dress counter to the stereotypes, practicing different ways to interrupt an oppressive joke or comment, role playing various ways of handling a racist boss without getting fired, challenging homophobia, strategizing how to build personal allies who will defend against abuse or speak out about discrimination.

ORGANIZING TO ELIMINATE. *Helping to challenge and eliminate oppression, as individuals, as a program, as a community.* Certainly, we have to help individual young people understand, heal from, and survive the current oppressive system better, but we also need to be thinking, acting, and organizing to kill the beast. YouthBuild USA takes the firm position that oppression can and must be eliminated. It won't happen in our lifetimes, to be sure, but we have to fight this fight. So the question is how can we help the young people become more skilled, committed, and engaged in eliminating oppression. Doing the first three things above will help, but what kinds of organizing and alliance building can move it beyond survival to action for real change?

How can we involve young people in local campaigns against issues of injustice and oppression? How can we support their moves to make change?

Challenges

This framework has some typical challenges, especially for staff working with young people in a program context. I would like to mention two. Let's take *informing*. There is much diversity among staff, even if each staff is from the same ethnic or racial background. Staff will have often have religious, political, and value differences among them. They may not agree about the roots of oppression, the value of diversity, or the goals of liberation. They may be teaching young people different things, which can be confusing to young people.

This is understandable given the range of opinions and positions in the wider world. For example, within the African American community of scholars, positions run the gamut from preaching full integration to emigrating to Africa. So here are some questions. What are we teaching young people about oppression and diversity? How do we get staff talking about these issues? How can staff engage in honest dialogue about their differences? Does a program need to have a unified stance or can diverse opinions co-exist? What are the implications of both? This takes a proactive leadership.

Another challenge is the *healing* part of the framework. Why is it that staff do not easily provide the safety and encouragement for young people to release their feelings about oppression? The main reason, in my opinion, is that we staff have a load of those same feelings that we have not healed. Stirring them up in young people risks stirring them up in ourselves. Few of us want to feel the level of rage or despair or fear or loss that we've managed and kept at bay for so long. Many YouthBuild staff are themselves only a step or two removed from the same conditions that the young people face. Their feelings are just below the surface. They face discrimination and disrespect most days themselves. So managing feelings has been a key to survival and getting as far as they have. We are not eager to surface all that.

In addition, most programs have no common methodology or process for dealing with staff emotions. So, again, here some questions to consider. How could we make it safe enough for staff to share their own experiences with discrimination, disrespect, and abuse due to some form of oppression? What if we could learn to build support groups into our work? What if we could practice listening deeply to each other and provide space for healing the wounds of racism, or sexism, or poverty, or antigay hostility, or adultism, and so on?

These two challenges—providing young people with a coherent picture of oppression, and making it safe enough to do some of the healing—are not easy for staff to do. Sometimes it helps to bring in a skilled outside facilitator experienced in these matters to guide the staff through discussions and sharing. Programs that have done good work on diversity issues have almost always started with the staff doing some of their own work together first. Young people depend on staff to set the tone. Young people are hungry for a safe environment that respects them, helps them grow, allows them to heal their hurts in an appropriate way, and offers them a holistic framework for liberating themselves from the misinformation, scars, and patterns due to oppression. This is work well worth training ourselves to do.

NOTE: For more resources on this topic, see my handbook *Creating a Diverse Community in YouthBuild,* available on the YouthBuild USA website, www.YouthBuild.org.

A positive approach to substance abuse

Use of drugs and alcohol is widespread among YouthBuild young people. The causes and conditions for this are complex. YouthBuild programs have various approaches to dealing with the prevalent use of substances by YouthBuild students. There is no silver bullet. What follows is a framework that I developed a few years back when I organized a symposium for YouthBuild staff and directors and experts on the subject. The staff then, and staff I have presented it to since, have found it a helpful guide. The first half is the wider historical perspective. The second part is the adaptation to the YouthBuild program. In staff trainings, often I go through it line by line and ask for comments and discussion. This approach might be used with your staff.

At the societal level

1. People have always used substances to change the way they feel and see the world.

2. Thus the idea of a drug-free world is probably a dream.

3. So the aim of public policy should be not to punish but to reduce harm.

4. Drugs should include tobacco, solvents, and over-the-counter drugs.

5. Illegal drugs have been demonized; users are considered evil and a threat to society.

6. Racism has fueled this depiction of users, resulting in greater incarceration of people of color.

7. Illegal drugs are a big business that operates like any big business: with great competition and profit.

8. Halting importation, production, and sale of illegal drugs has proved nearly impossible.

9. Thus, the "war on drugs" has been a huge waste of public monies.

10. Use of illegal drugs cuts across all segments of population, all social classes and locations.

11. The majority of illegal drug use is of marijuana; its use is relatively moderate and managed by most users, though chronic use can certainly cause dysfunction and dependency.

12. Why do people use drugs: to have fun, enjoy the company of others, or relieve pain, and even as a means of spiritual enlightenment. Some are physically addicted and need them. Some just experiment with them.

13. Some people become dependent—again, across all sections of society.

14. Alcohol and tobacco cause far more harm than marijuana.

15. Yet illegal drug policy centers on crime and punishment rather than on education and prevention.

16. Public policy needs to shift to reducing harm, informing people about the risks, encouraging no use while emphasizing sensible safe use if used at all.

17. Treatment should include a wide range of services to meet drug users needs: employment, housing, medical and mental health needs, and so on.

18. Four main types of therapeutic treatment are 12-step, behavioral, family-based, and therapeutic communities.

19. Research on these types of treatment with adolescents shows that:

- Treatment works if people stay with it, though no treatment method stands out as superior.

- Relapse rate is high, given the power of the youth culture and peer pressure.

- Dropout rate in treatment programs is high, from 20 to 50 percent.

- Substance abuse is a complex problem needing multiple approaches to fit the person, but health insurance and managed care work against matching care to the needs of users.

20. Decriminalize drug use. Pursue organized crime for selling illegal drugs.

21. Take the moral judgment out of drug policy; emphasize consequences and reducing harm.

At the YouthBuild program level

1. 70 to 80 percent of YouthBuild young people use substances, according to the rate of dirty tests in program drug tests.

2. YouthBuild students are caught in a cultural double message regarding marijuana or other illegal substances: your friends say you're a punk if you don't use and the society and employers say you're a criminal if you do.

3. Some young people are addicted, for sure, and need help. The program can help.

4. Most young people use moderately and recreationally, but can't pass employer or program drug tests, so they are at risk of losing their jobs or spots in the program. Therefore, if the program is committed to helping young people find and retain high-paying, living-wage jobs, it must have a serious approach to drug use.

5. Some elements of one successful approach by a YouthBuild program:

- Drug testing is not used to screen applicants, since most young people use drugs.

- Relationships are built before testing (young people need to know they have support to reduce or stop).

- Establish clear program policy during orientation (for example, YouthBuild is a drug-free environment; there is help available; students must sign a statement saying they will be drug-free and that they understand they will be randomly tested. Testing is to prepare for living-wage jobs, not for punishment or morality purposes.)

- Serious drug and alcohol education takes place at beginning of program, and throughout the program.

- Begin random drug testing four to six weeks into the program, and continue weekly (3 people per week).

- If the test is dirty, the student is referred to drug education partner for assessment (is it serious addiction or not?) and determination of treatment (is residential or outpatient program better?)

- If residential, stipend is paid to student while in the residential program.

- If outpatient treatment, student continues to attend program but not the worksite activities other than tasks like sweeping, due to safety issues, until a clean drug test is achieved.

- Persistent caring from counselor or other staff is essential for success.

6. Help each young person to create a "personal drug-free zone" in which each person:

- Asks *Who am I and how do drugs help or hinder who I am?*

- Explores the effect of drugs on his or her body, mind, heart, spirit, and family

- Builds up a vision of a successful life, maximizing potential

- Gets honest about use or addiction; admits it; stops denying; asks for help

- Learns about the nature of hurt, habits, and healing

- Comes to see how drug use is reinforced by racism and poverty

- Creates a personal plan for success: goals, steps, obstacles, support, rewards, etc.

- Begins a balanced program of goals for heart, mind, body, spirit (see page 153)

- Uses the YouthBuild program to help; counselor, staff, and student support

- Celebrates each small step, each accomplishment

7. Establish a "program drug-free zone." Build a positive, supportive community as a strong alternative to the drug culture, including:

- Meaningful work for the students

- A culture of transformation that includes healing, learning, challenge, high expectations, self-discipline, rituals, a positive community

- Leadership development, engaging young people in decision making

- Caring and competent staff that never give up on young people

- A positive peer culture

- Real help with real problems

- Relevant and marketable skills development

- A clear pathway to a brighter future, with effort and persistence

- Consistency in tone, expectations, ground rules, discipline, procedures

- Ongoing policy, assessment, goal setting, and challenge about individual drug use

To reiterate: Substance use and abuse is complex. It lies at the intersection of individual, cultural, and societal forces. It involves personal hurts, social oppression, strong habits and addiction, and confused attempts to achieve happiness and contentedness. There is no simple one-size-fits-all drug policy for YouthBuild programs. Ideally, a program's staff would be open to the framework outlined above and to continually help to implement numbers 6 and 7, concerning personal drug-free zones and building a positive program drug-free zone, respectively.

The systemic use of appreciation

Most young people in a YouthBuild program carry with them various hurts from their personal lives, from racism or from growing up poor. The damage shows up in various ways in different people: feelings of self-doubt, lack of confidence, powerlessness; appearing stupid or lazy or irresponsible; acting out feelings of anger, disrespect, meanness, hostility, violence, etc. These feelings and behaviors interfere with people's abilities to learn, to think, to set and achieve goals, to be leaders.

A YouthBuild program is not a therapeutic community and may not be able to help with the deepest of these scars, but a constant dose of genuine appreciation and approval can go a long way in counteracting some of the damage. A thoroughgoing practice of appreciation in all parts of the program helps build a nurturing and positive environment in which young people and staff can learn better, feel supported, and make better decisions.

Below are some suggested methods of doing appreciations. In Youth-Build we have the most experience with the kinds of appreciations listed in number one. We know this format works. We have less experience with self-appreciation, as suggested in practice number 2, but it is extremely important to keep trying. The other methods listed have been used in different places and are worth experimenting with.

1) Regular appreciations. Regular and frequent appreciations should be standard practice—at the end of the day, at the end of a meeting, at the end of a conflict, etc. These are public and done one at a time so that everybody can hear what is said to each person.

Some variations include (change names and other details as appropriate, of course):

- *Say one thing you like about the person on your left.* (or right, or two people to your left or right, or the person directly across from you).

- *Let's have appreciations from the people on either side of you.*

- *What did so and so do today that helped...* (...the class, the worksite, the meeting, etc.)?

- *What do you respect or admire about Derrick?*

- *What makes Cassandra a valuable part of YouthBuild?*

- *How have you seen Jose grow in the last few months?*

- *How has Mary been a good leader...* (...this week, or lately, or on this job, etc.)?

2) Self-appreciations. It is often more difficult for people to validate themselves than to accept praise from others, but it is a crucial step in building self-confidence and self-esteem. It is good to begin this privately since people have a lot of conditioning against bragging and feel too embarrassed or exposed to do it in public. But you need to talk with the whole group about the importance of appreciating themselves, and to help each other learn to do it.

Examples include:

- *What do you like about yourself?*

- *Tell us a time when you felt very intelligent.* (or brave, sensitive, generous, strong, funny, loving, successful, etc.)

- *What obstacles are you proud of overcoming in your life?*

- *What are your biggest accomplishments?*

- *When did you stand up for somebody? Tell the story.*

- *Times you were a leader?*

- *Times you helped another person? Tell the story.*

- *What do you like about yourself as an African American man?* (or as a woman, or as a young person, or as an Irish young person, or as a Native American person, etc. depending on their background)

- *What makes you proud of being an African-American man?* (etc., as above)

- *What would you like others to appreciate about you?,* etc.

3) A validation game. Privately say to a young person, "I am thinking of something I really like about you. Guess what it is. You get three guesses." After three guesses, tell them. The student will enjoy it, since they have to appreciate themselves while guessing, in addition to getting your validation of them if they don't guess. You will also get a lot of good information about them through their guesses. Pay attention to what they say. They are giving you big clues about themselves, either what they like about themselves or what they want someone else to notice.

After doing this privately for a while with various young people, try a public variation: ask other students to guess what you are thinking about so-and-so. (Be prepared to quickly interrupt any negative put-downs.)

4) 3 x 5 appreciation stack. Focusing on one student a week, have the other students write a private appreciation of that person on a three-by-five-inch index card and put it in a box anonymously. The selected person gets to keep the stack, and can read the cards privately or share them as she or he wishes. Repeat this activity throughout the year. (Staff needs to review cards and remove any jokes or insults before student reads them.)

5) Appreciation wall charts. After enough safety has been established so that put-downs and insults are rare, put up a piece of newsprint or oak tag for each trainee, with his or her name at the top. Focusing on a different student every day or every week, ask the other students what they like about him or her. Write what they say on the wall chart until it is filled. Leave the charts up for a long time.

6) Guess who? Each student picks another student's name from a hat and writes down something outstanding or some positive or good quality about that person. Then the student reads aloud what he wrote and the rest of the group tries to guess who it was written about. Variations are limited only to the imagination.

On the next page is a wonderful self-appreciation that can serve as a reminder of our inherent nature. Print it out. Pass it out. Put it up everywhere. Talk about it. Recite it often. Use it as a steady reminder of the transformation we are after! (The words are taken from my article "A Process of Emotional Healing." After reading the article, the words will make more sense. The list was put into a graphic format by former YouthBuild director, Pamela Beckwith. (You can download a printable version at http://northstar.link/appreciationchart.)

By nature, all humans are...

Inherently Valuable

Enormously Intelligent

Deeply Caring

Immensely Powerful

Infinitely Creative

Naturally Cooperative

Innately Joyful

9

Construction's Role in Leadership Development

C onstruction is not my area of expertise, and there are wonderful resources for the construction component of YouthBuild.
(See the handbook *Construction Training at a YouthBuild Program* and unit 4 of the *Working Hands, Working Minds curriculum.*)
My purpose in this brief chapter is to make a few links between construction and the vision of YouthBuild as a transformational leadership-development program.

CONSTRUCTION AS A
METAPHOR FOR TRANSFORMATION

First, we all know that young people often see "building the house" as
a metaphor for building their lives. They say things like *Yeah, we tear
out all these old pipes and put new ones back in. Sorta like me. The program is helping me take out the old habits and put back ones that work
better.* YouthBuild focuses on the construction of affordable housing
for many reasons:

- Building affordable housing is a lasting and needed contribution to community development and poverty alleviation.

- A construction site teaches good work skills: timeliness, safety, follow-through, completion, striving towards quality work.

- A construction site cannot operate without teamwork; people learn to depend on each other.

- Building a house has a logic to it ("critical path management," as it is called in the business) that teaches young people planning, estimating, sequencing, coordinating, and timing of a project—skills applicable to many parts of life.

- Learning basic construction skills makes young people more marketable if they choose to work in the construction field.

- The skills learned will be useful over a lifetime; even if a young person does not go on in construction, he or she will always be able to fix things around the house, or even earn a little side money repairing, say, Ms. Jones's front porch.

- Building or rebuilding a house gives young people a tangible, substantive sense of accomplishment.

- Seeing a formerly homeless family move into a house they built fills the hearts of the young people with pride and shows them the importance of community service.

- The work they do is visible in the community to their peers and family, producing a positive ripple effect.

CONSTRUCTION AS HUMAN DEVELOPMENT

The house can also be the "therapy room," as staff at Operation Fresh Start YouthBuild in Madison, Wisconsin, call it. Because of the teamwork and hands-on nature of the construction site, and because construction staff also take on the roles of teachers and mentors, lots of one-to-one bonding often happens on the worksite. Many young people come to feel safe with their construction trainers, and it is not uncommon for a student to confide in a construction staff during break time up on the roof. This is why, ideally, construction staff are hired for their human relations abilities as much as their technical know-how. This is why they should be considered teachers and counselors as much as they are considered construction staff. This is why they need ongoing training in effective listening. The construction staff can teach life skills, support the academic side, tag-team with the counselor, help with job placements, and foster leadership.

CONSTRUCTION STAFF AND LEADERSHIP DEVELOPMENT

Construction staff as leaders. In the vision of YouthBuild promoted in this book, the construction staff play key roles in the development of young leaders. First, as I said in chapter 5, Building a Strong and Cohesive Staff, I would hire construction staff who were leaders in their lives. Maybe they are active in the local trade union, belong to a community organization, or have worked on a political campaign. They would need to understand that their job is to help develop young leaders *through* the construction work, that leadership development is not something that is done on top of construction or after hours. They would set up the work so that young people rotated through real leadership roles.

Critical questions. As the students worked on a site, construction staff would ask critical questions to promote real discussion, like: Why do you think there are so many broken down houses in the community? Why do people become homeless? Was this always a low-income neighborhood? How many people on this block own their homes? Who else owns them? What kinds of stores and businesses are in the neighborhood and why? Where are the safe places for children to play? If you were mayor, what would you do to improve the community? And so on.

Environmental awareness. Since an ever-increasing number of programs are doing green building, the construction staff, reinforced by the academic staff, would help develop the environmental awareness of the students. Not only would they address how to build with green materials or position a house for best use of the natural shade and wind protections, but they'd also discuss issues like climate change, global warming, and environmental justice. Regular conversations or classes could focus on questions such as: What can young people and their families could do to conserve energy and water, consume less, recycle more? What local, state, and national policies would help us green our lives? Why is it important to vote for candidates who propose to curb climate change and stop environmental injustice? What is the connection between your children's asthma and the coal-fired power plant a mile away? The goal might be to help some of the students become green educators for their communities, being the neighborhood equivalent of Al Gore bringing an adapted version of *An Inconvenient Truth* to the hood!

Pride in working people. The construction staff could also educate young people about the history of working people, the struggles of unions to improve conditions, the pride in the fact that working people built the country, literally! All the roads, bridges, buildings, railroads, airports, cell-phone towers, power lines, oil refineries—everything!

Leadership development processes on the worksite. The list below outlines some best practices of leadership development through the construction component. These practices are detailed in the *Construction Training at a YouthBuild Program* handbook.

Leadership Development at the **Construction Worksite**

Young people:

- Rotate leadership roles (for example, act in turn as crew chief, safety coordinator, tool captain, site steward (responsible for calling for breaks, cleanup, attendance), or as the person who makes supply store runs or takes photographs to document work)
- Attend contract negotiations or go to city hall to pull permits
- Help plan, estimate materials for, and create schedule for work projects
- Conduct tours for site visitors
- Learn why green building is important, become leaders on environmental issues
- Evaluate the construction staff and each other

A standard practice might also be to sit down as a work crew at the end of each week and assess the week's work. *What did we do well this week? What could be improved? What did you learn? What new ideas did you have? What did I do well as a supervisor? How could I improve? How well did we function as a team? How could we improve our teamwork? How was Jamiel (and each student in turn) a leader on the worksite this week? Whom do you want to appreciate?* And so on. The construction staff sees these regular meetings as opportunities to build the group cohesion, teach good group process, highlight effective leadership, and deepen learning—all part of overall leadership development. Everything speaks!

NOTE. In this chapter I have only focused on the traditional construction aspect of the YouthBuild vocational training, but, of course, similar principles and approaches apply to health care, nursing, information technology, and other vocational pathways offered by various YouthBuild programs.

10

Graduate Resources

$\mathcal{E}$ ven if a YouthBuild program implements a quality critical thinking education process, a deep emotional healing process, and a rich leadership development process, as recommended throughout this book, it is obvious to anyone who knows YouthBuild young people that graduation is not the end of the transformation. A few graduates might be prepared to make it on their own, but most have barely begun to lay down new habits and attitudes, root out negative thinking, build a positive peer network, and make realistic goals for their success. Ten to twelve months is just the beginning. Furthermore, a scarce-job economy, a family crisis, or the lure of fast money in street life can cause a young person to backslide and undo the progress made during YouthBuild. Longtime YouthBuild directors and staff can tell story after story of young people coming back three or four years later to thank them for providing the spark, and to share what the journey has been since leaving YouthBuild—typically with arduous setbacks countered by their resilience and persistence.

In addition, there is the loss of potential *collective* impact. When we step back from the daily work and put YouthBuild in a world context, as we have touched on in earlier chapters, it is clear to me that we are in a historic period of breakdown or breakthrough—our political and economic systems are broken, our people are suffering, and the earth is hurting. New kinds of leadership are needed at all levels, including leadership from people in low-income communities who are most negatively affected by the breakdowns. In the United States, there are about 7,000 new YouthBuild graduates each year. Over 10 years that's 70,000—a huge potential "force for good." But we are squandering this potential resource by not organizing strong local graduate networks. Right now, this potential evaporates after graduation. The huge investment made through the program year is weakened and mostly lost as a collective potential. This is an unsolved and urgent challenge before us.

To maximize the enormous potential of YouthBuild young people, and to extend the impact of the YouthBuild experience, it is vital to build a robust graduate-resources component that engages graduates and extends the supportive environment for as long as is needed. This is not just a fine idea if it can be funded. It is essential.

Graduate success, after all is said and done, is why we are doing Youth-Build. The elements of graduate success are straightforward. When asked, almost every group of YouthBuild staff or students or graduates comes up with a list similar to this:

Benchmarks of graduate success
- Pursuing postsecondary education or credential
- Building towards or maintaining a well-paying and satisfying career
- Creating a positive family, personal, and social-support network
- Engaging in community affairs
- Caring for emotional and physical health
- Building financial assets

RECONCEIVING YOUTHBUILD AS
A MULTIYEAR TRANSFORMATION PROCESS

It might be useful to step back and re-envision YouthBuild. Currently, we tend to think of YouthBuild as a *program* that lasts six to twelve months, with a nine-month follow-up period for DOL-funded programs, with deliverables and performance measures within that timeframe. After graduation, there are a limited number of supports, for programs that have funding for it. Even though we decry the situation, typically graduates are mostly on their own in a cold, heartless world and a bad economy, while staff turn their attention to the new group of students coming in the front door, since this is so demanding in itself, and it's where the funding requires staff to focus. The funders—federal, corporate, and foundations—have a similar short-term-solution way of thinking about social services rather than investing in long-term substantive change processes.

To propose a new approach: What if we re-conceived of YouthBuild not as a *program* that lasted a few months, but as a *process of change* that lasted a few years? The program as we currently know it would be phase one, with a lively and more varied graduate phase following graduation, as the sketch below indicates. Beginning with end in mind—young people able to sustain their transformational process toward achieving their goals and contributing to the community — we will want to design and resource the graduate phase to be as well thought-out as the program phase, with staff, funding, data, follow-up, and so on. We can approach funders and the community with this longer-range view of YouthBuild. Below is a diagram of what a group of experienced YouthBuild directors came up with when I asked them how they would conceptualize YouthBuild if they had adequate funding and capacity.

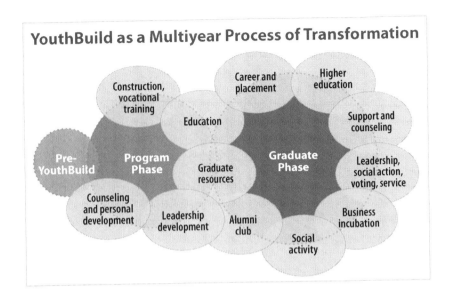

Youthbuild as a Multiyear Process of Transformation

YouthBuild as a Multiyear Process of Transformation

After the first two years of a YouthBuild program, graduates would outnumber program students. The graduate phase of YouthBuild would eventually grow to be larger and more varied than the program phase.

Admittedly, this would be a major shift in our current conception of YouthBuild—and a shift not easy to make, since the government and other funders are wedded to a business model of quantifiable deliverables and results within a given timeframe. But intuitively we know that an extended transformational support context is more realistic and would lead to even higher program outcomes and individual successes.

Current funder focus on performance has in fact raised outcomes. This is in the right direction but doesn't extend long enough.

YouthBuild programs sometimes get stuck with an approach that goes something like this: at graduation, the program has a wonderful celebration, invites families and supporters, gives awards and diplomas to happy students dressed in caps and gowns, has a nice dinner, and exchanges heartfelt goodbyes to those students. After catching their breath, staff then turn toward the new students coming in the door, because the new class requires their full attention. They stay in touch with graduates as much as possible, and maybe offer a few services or events. But 95 percent of their attention is turned toward the new group. Meanwhile the recent graduates are trying to make their way in the world of work or school or family issues mostly on their own, without the support of their YouthBuild staff.

Neither staff nor graduates like this situation. Program directors know they should be providing deeper ongoing support to graduates, and would like to. Even when funding allows for or requires student follow-up for a number of months after completion, in reality, this follow-up is thin, consisting mostly of tracking graduate placements. Far from what is needed.

To make matters worse, staff turnover is often higher than desirable, resulting in returning graduates not being able to find the staff who had mentored them, not being able to connect with the caring adults they had come to trust, even when they take the initiative to seek them out. This issue of staff turnover deserves special attention in itself toward program quality and graduate connection. I have not tried to address it here beyond mentioning it.

Now consider this. If YouthBuild Anytown (harkening back to the idealized YouthBuild program first mentioned in chapter 6) graduates 30 students this year, a year from now there are 60 graduates, two years from now, 90 graduates, and so on. Soon there are many more graduates than current students, but hardly any funds for graduate programming. This makes no sense in terms of maximizing graduate success and graduate leadership roles.

Some programs have been able to overcome this situation and provide a solid graduate phase. In recent years, for example, the Youth-Build USA Postsecondary Education Initiative, funded by the Bill

& Melinda Gates Foundation, Open Society Foundations, and New Profit Inc. through YouthBuild USA to local programs, has greatly increased success in college and apprenticeships and has created a support network for graduates involved in this. We hope this successful work grows. Much deeper graduate support work is called for in more sites than these pilot sites.

A VISION OF GRADUATE RESOURCES AT YOUTHBUILD ANYTOWN

What follows is a vision of a well-developed YouthBuild graduate-resources program. It is one of many possible models. It assumes ideal conditions: adequate funding; a seamless connection to the first year program phase; excellent staffing; a variety of well-conceived and implemented components; commitment from board, staff, and participants; and a solid connection with the local community. This vision also assumes that the program has two and one-half years of operation under its belt. No YouthBuild program has yet incorporated all of the elements described below, although some programs have developed some of the ideas included. This vision is intended to paint a positive picture and point to the possible.

~

YouthBuild Anytown's graduates

YouthBuild Anytown has been in existence for two and one-half years. There are 35 participants in the current cycle, and 62 graduates from the previous two cycles. Already the current students have been preparing for what comes after graduation. They were told at the beginning of their orientation that their contact with YouthBuild does not have to end with graduation, that there is a second phase of YouthBuild for graduates. They have been preparing their résumés, learning job-readiness skills, developing good work and study habits, learning how to achieve their personal goals. Some of them will soon begin short-term apprenticeships with employers outside YouthBuild to accustom them to new job settings and to extend their skill development. And they see graduates around YouthBuild every day, including some who are on staff.

Of the 62 graduates, about 45 regularly participate in graduate-program activities. The program is deliberately designed to be flexible enough to accommodate graduates at whatever level of time and interest they have. Before they graduate, all students are thoroughly and frequently briefed about the opportunities and services of the graduate program. After graduation, graduates receive regular mailings about graduate activities, and personal phone calls to see how they are doing and inviting them to come.

Graduate education services
Some graduates utilize the graduate-education resources. For example, some graduates didn't complete their high school equivalency while in the program, so they come back for regular prep classes taught by their former teacher. They help each other study and arrange to take the tests on the same day for mutual support. Other graduates have decided to go on to higher education and return to the program to get help visiting local community colleges or universities, and filling out the admissions and financial aid forms. Others have been in college for several months and need tutoring help or encouragement to stick with it. Older college students have been enlisted as volunteers to tutor the YouthBuild graduates. The education component also has relationships with the local trade schools and community colleges that are eager to accept serious YouthBuild graduates and help them find financial aid if needed. And, finally, occasionally a course is offered through the graduate program taught by a board member, staff, or community person. Graduates have been able to take classes in basic accounting, word processing, and parenting skills.

Job resources at YouthBuild Anytown

Since the number-one need of most graduates is to earn the money they need to live, the YouthBuild graduate program puts major emphasis on job resources. There is a job bank—a regularly updated list of jobs available or employers who have hired YouthBuild graduates previously. The job counselor/developer is available to talk with graduates who have lost jobs to help them determine why, and if there are things they can do next time to avoid losing the job. Graduates can use the program's computers to revise their resumes or write cover letters to prospective employers. When there is a group of job seekers, the job counselor will have them do job-interview role-plays to get practice and peer feedback in preparation for the real thing. The job developer and the executive director of the agency sponsoring YouthBuild make personal relationships with a wide range of employers and get commitments for job slots for YouthBuild graduates. The program has also offered two 40-hour training certification courses in lead abatement, asbestos removal, and toxic-waste handling. The program also employs a graduate from the first cycle as an assistant construction trainer and alumni coordinator.

The graduate program also has a small-business incubation project. An experienced staff person provides technical assistance, training, and support for graduates who want to start their own businesses. There is a revolving loan fund to provide startup capital. So far, this project has helped launch three successful businesses of graduates: a home day-care business, a floor-polishing business, and a house-painting company.

Alternatively, the program manages a small business itself, which provides weatherization services to the community and hires graduates to perform the work. This produces a small revenue stream for the program, but more importantly provides a second stage of employment experience for graduates who have not found employment elsewhere.

Graduate support

A good number of graduates find the personal counseling and social services essential from time to time. A graduate counselor is available to help a graduate through a crisis, act as a good listener, be an advocate with the welfare or the justice system, assist in finding better housing, or help a graduate deal with any number of ongoing personal issues which don't stop when a person graduates from Youth-Build. The counselor is someone the graduates knew when they were students, so there is already a level of trust and confidence built up.

Some graduates also maintain the support groups which began during the program cycle. There is a support group for young parents, a group for men, and a 12-step program for graduates recovering from substance abuse. These are mostly peer-led but the counselor offers his professional knowledge and skills as a member of these groups.

There is a graduate-mentoring program. Currently 38 graduates have mentors—people from the community or among the employees of corporate partners who volunteer to attend to a graduate's further development, which include weekly face to face meetings, regular phone calls or social media contacts that may take the form of, coaching, opening doors of opportunity, being a sounding board, giving advice, and caring personally about the well-being and future of the graduate. The graduate program staff takes care to match people well and to have periodic reviews of the mentoring relationships. This mentoring program is based on the model developed by YouthBuild USA under the OJJDP funding since 2009, through which over 60 programs have received funding.

Graduate activities

Since the majority of the graduates are working full-time or are in college, most of the YouthBuild graduate activities take place in the evenings or on weekends. After trying various staffing patterns over the past several years, YouthBuild Anytown now has one full-time graduate program coordinator who works evening and weekends, and the part-time services of a GED instructor, a counselor, and a job developer. In addition, there are two graduates hired each year as interns to help coordinate the graduate program. The budget includes staff salaries, activity money (which also covers related meals and snacks), and asset-trust funds for gifts to graduates. This is built into YouthBuild Anytown's funding proposals from the beginning.

Graduate funding

Gifts to Graduates, a fund for graduates, was fashioned after the Asset Trust Fund that YouthBuild USA had developed for graduates and the needs-based fund that is allowed by DOL for current students. Graduates can apply for a small grant if they face unexpected crises such as the death of a parent, the illness of a child, or a car accident, or they find an unexpected opportunity that requires a small amount of money to pursue, such as an invitation to participate in an overseas study tour, or to attend a training conference, or get a job that requires owning a car or more tools. These gifts can be decisive in the graduates' lives and are the kinds of gifts that parents with means would give their children. But since our graduates typically do not have parents who can support them in this way, YouthBuild has found this model to be extremely helpful for graduates.

Graduate leadership, development, and service

As does the program cycle, the graduate program has its own policy committee. Six members are elected by the graduates. They meet once a month with the graduate program coordinator to take part in hiring any new graduate program staff, iron out program difficulties, set new directions, and give the coordinator advice.

Graduates are encouraged to keep developing themselves and their leadership. Innumerable leadership opportunities are made available to graduates. Two graduates serve on YouthBuild Anytown's board of directors. Graduates are called upon to accompany the director on fundraising events, to be spokespersons for YouthBuild at community meetings, to talk to the media, and to recruit and select new students.

There is a graduate alumni club whose activities are graduate-led and determined by the interests of the members. YouthBuild Anytown's alumni club has decided to put attention on three things: community service and civic engagement, a positive social life, and organizing a community youth conference.

For community service, this year on Thanksgiving they collected food at Thanksgiving for the local homeless shelter. Three graduates who work at night volunteer in the neighborhood elementary school during the day to help teach reading to second graders. In the recent Presidential election, a core of alumni volunteered to register voters and get them to the polls to increase voting rates. Also, several graduates serve on the parent-teacher association, and one graduate is running for the local school committee.

Graduate gatherings
To continue the positive social life they began before graduation, the alumni club has organized monthly events: barbecues, bowling parties, ball games, pizza parties with children. They have also organized a YouthBuild basketball team and entered into the city league. They encourage graduates to hang out with each other to reinforce the positive choices they learned to make during the program year. Such social activities have been an important anchor in the lives of many graduates.

The YouthBuild alumni club also organized a youth conference in the community. They felt it was important to get other young people and young adults together to listen to each other define the problems they face in the community and the solutions they proposed. It took six months of work to pull it off. About a dozen alumni club members took the lead. They called other agencies, spoke at school assemblies, got PSAs on the local radio shows, and spread the word on the street that the conference was happening. They invited the mayor, other public officials, and the media to attend and listen. They got the public-access TV station to tape the whole thing. They had youth speakers and facilitators. In the end, the conference drew over 200 people. It was a good beginning discussion of issues facing youth and what could be done about them. The alumni club wrote up a summary of the recommendations that emerged from the meeting and distributed them throughout the community and then presented them to public officials. They got tremendous appreciation for initiating such a conference. It was an important leadership experience for the members. This was actively supported by the program director and sponsoring organization.

Graduates are also plugged into the national YouthBuild USA graduate network. Encouraged by the program before graduation, most have signed up to receive regular communication from YouthBuild USA that announces upcoming leadership opportunities, internships, and events; highlights recent successes of graduates; or asks graduates for their opinions on various matters. Many of them are part of the YouthBuild 1000 Leaders Network, which allows them to attend the annual national YouthBuild Alumni Xchange (AX) conference. Most check in on the YouthBuild USA Alumni Facebook page to keep in touch with other young leaders they met at the AX. One graduate is serving a three-year term as a member of the National Alumni Council, which is elected at the AX. Several joined the YouthBuild National Speakers Bureau and have been called on to give testimony or be on a panel at a national event. Several graduates have gotten placements through one of YouthBuild USA partners—VISTA, NCCC, Public Allies, or Year Up.

Overall, the YouthBuild Anytown graduate program is a vibrant center of activity, learning, new challenges, support, and that "family feeling" that graduates had while in the program phase of YouthBuild. *Once in YouthBuild, always in YouthBuild!* They can build on the hard-won growth they accomplished during the program phase. The graduate program even provides child care for many of the activities, to make it easier for the parents. Graduates still feel that YouthBuild Anytown is home where they can have continuing contact with staff who cared about them during the program phase, be around positive peers, be inspired by the vision of YouthBuild in the community. The overarching themes are continuing self-development, leadership development, community development, and continued involvement in YouthBuild.

～

Obviously, the above vision of a fully developed graduate phase of the YouthBuild experience, however desirable, is beyond the present capacity of most YouthBuild programs. To move in this direction, which is the heartfelt wish of most YouthBuild directors that I have talked with, we will need to cultivate an expanded notion of what YouthBuild is—a multiyear change process instead of a six- to twelve-month program; raise money to support the graduate phase by enlisting funders in this expanded vision; experiment with many structures and staffing patterns of the graduate phase and share the learning across the network; and do a longitudinal study of the impact on the lives of young people who go through such an extended YouthBuild experience. This is a long-range project, but one that we might as well begin now.

A 2003 study of YouthBuild graduates commissioned by YouthBuild USA and performed by Brandeis University reported that a strong recommendation from the graduates in the study was for greater graduate engagement. More recently, the 2013 National Alumni Council called for attention to creating a context that continues to welcome and engage graduates, with greater continuity of staff.

Recommendations for building your graduate network

Developing strong graduate work is a continuing challenge, but one that is vital for two reasons stated in the first part of this chapter: One is to provide a longer engagement between YouthBuild and individual graduates so that they can solidify the gains they made in the program phase and have a much greater chance of success. The other reason is to bring to reality that the potential collective force that graduates represent for good in the community. As a network, we have not yet figured out how to mount and sustain robust graduate programs. If we did know how, we would do it. So I am proposing that we make this a networkwide campaign for the foreseeable future. Let's try every good idea and see what works. Here are some elements that occur to me.

1. **New conception of YouthBuild.** Begin to think of YouthBuild as a multiyear process of transformation along the lines outlined in the opening section of this chapter. From the orientation forward, let young people know that YouthBuild is more than a six-, nine-, or twelve-month program. Let them know that there are graduate resources, activities, and supports for them as long as they need them—a home base, a positive peer community, an incubator for their growth and dreams. Keep telling them that *Once in Youth-Build, always in YouthBuild.* Show them all the ways they can stay involved after graduation from phase one. Introduce them to the YouthBuild USA graduate Facebook page.

2. **Visioning.** As part of reconceiving YouthBuild, the board, staff, students, and graduates should be engaged in developing a vision of what a full-bodied graduate resources phase of YouthBuild would look like. The input of graduates is especially crucial since they have been out in the world of work and schooling and know what supports would help most.

3. **Dedicated staffing.** Hire a staff person to coordinate and build the graduate work. Start slow, but start. The process might need to be part-time at first for funding reasons, but finding a person dedicated to this work for the long term is extremely important. Some programs have assigned graduate outreach to a VISTA or Ameri-Corps student, but this is usually insufficient because that person leaves after a year, and the relationships leave with that person, as often does the momentum. Long-term staff are need to be able to carry out the vision.

4. **Promote program involvement.** Even before you have a vision or even dedicated staff, you can begin by finding every opportunity to invite graduates back to the program to help with recruitment, talk with students, lead some Mental Toughness exercises, share work or college successes with current students, advise the new policy committee, mentor younger leaders, talk at fundraising events, lead workshops, organize a poetry slam or music jam, use the computer lab after hours, and so on. At first this takes active attention. Ask the question: What could a graduate do better than I could as director or staff? Make graduates feel especially welcomed when they come back to the program. Make time to talk with them, even though you are busy. Train new staff to welcome graduates, even when they don't know them.

5. **Start with most recent graduates.** If you have graduates, invite them back for a think-tank session on building what they need in the way of graduate support. (Call it whatever will bring them in.) Most graduates have busy lives with work, school, family, or other responsibilities. They need their time respected, like all of us. So ask them to think with you about what would be valuable enough for them to stay involved with YouthBuild. Job help? Social activities? Parenting groups? Postsecondary education help? Mentoring? Sporting events? Community service opportunities? Fun? Interesting internships? Political engagement to create social change in the neighborhood? Follow their lead; provide these activities as much as possible. If they are well-done and positive, the word will spread to other graduates that YouthBuild has something to offer them.

6. **Personalize the contact.** Relationships are at the heart of any successful graduate follow-up. As they did in the program phase, graduates need to feel cared for and respected. Thus, people they knew and had good relationships with during the program are the best ones to reach out and stay in contact with them after graduation. Graduates have told us that when so many staff leave, and

they don't know anyone at YouthBuild anymore, they have little incentive to check in with the program. When they visit and
nobody pays special attention, there's no point in returning. So
continuity of caring staff is paramount. It is not always possible,
but it is optimal. Having a new VISTA reach out to graduates for
phone numbers or e-mails is not enough, and is no substitute for a
known caring staff member. One idea is to ask each staff to maintain contact with a subgroup of graduates for at least the first year
after graduation. An obvious but challenging subtask is to maintain an ever-growing contact database of graduates and communicate with them regularly with news of successes and announce-
ments of activities and opportunities. One YouthBuild director
told me that each day before going home, she contacts five graduates—a short Facebook "like", a text asking about the baby, a voice
message saying "I'm thinking about you. Just wanted to say hi;"
and so on.

7. **Cultivate graduate leaders.** Not all graduate work depends on the
YouthBuild staff, though it usually starts there. Even before graduation, the program might prepare and support key magnet leaders to be future organizers of graduate events. Graduates tend to
respond better to invitations from their known friends and Youth-
Build peers. One graduate I know used to have monthly pizza and
game nights at his house. Ideally, graduates would be welcomed to
use YouthBuild space, but it's not always required. Graduates can
get involved in a community issue of common concern. They can
educate each other about events in the world.

As we move in the direction of growing solid, robust graduate work, as
a network we will become more resourceful, inventive, and successful.
The point is to begin now.

We could, of course, settle for just running a good full-time program
for students who make lasting gains while they are with us. That is
worth doing. But it would seem to me to be a huge loss for society and

for our communities not to grow and harness the powerful energy to give back and make change that is generated by YouthBuild at its best.

LEADERSHIP DEVELOPMENT BENCHMARKS FOR SUCCESSFUL GRADUATES

Let us tie the graduate work back to leadership development. For individual graduates, if we use the leadership categories of "taking responsibility to make things go right for self, family, program, and community" to propose some benchmarks for a successful graduate, a set of benchmarks might look something like the list below. In implementing this, we might propose that two or three years after graduation, for example, a successful graduate accomplishes at least 75 percent of the following benchmarks.

SELF Leadership Benchmarks

- Has set a savings goal for the year and is actively saving money
- Keeps a calendar and is on time for appointments
- Is reliable; does what she or he promises to do
- Has regular healthy practices for body, mind, heart, and spirit (exercise, nutrition, sleep, health, stress reduction, spiritual connections, etc.)
- Has a regular "listening partner" to process emotional distress and gain clarity
- Has developed ways to regulate negative feelings so as to not be ruled by them
- Maintains regular contact with a mentor or life coach
- If struggling with substances, actively participates in AA, NA, or similar support network
- Has made investments in his or her education—college, trade school, certifications
- Other?

FAMILY Leadership Benchmarks

- If a parent, is actively engaged with his or her children each week
- Provides money and support to family members as possible
- Spends time with and mentors younger siblings and family members
- Attends child's PTA meetings, helps with homework
- Has resolved at least one ruptured family relationship
- Is saving to own his or her own home
- Other?

PROGRAM Leadership Benchmarks

"Program" includes both local YouthBuild programs and YouthBuild USA

- Keeps the program and YouthBuild USA informed of contact changes
- Contributes at least ten to fifty dollars a year to his or her local YouthBuild program
- Is available to program for talks to students, advocacy, fundraising
- Volunteers to mentor a current student
- Attends a YouthBuild alumni conference as often as possible
- Is a member of the YouthBuild USA 1000 Leaders Network
- Is part of the YouthBuild National Speakers Bureau
- Responds to requests to contact congressperson to support YouthBuild
- Other?

COMMUNITY Leadership Benchmarks

- If eligible, is registered to vote and votes in all local, state, and national elections
- Stays informed about community, national, and world events by reading regularly
- Is recognized as a role model for other young people
- Has been a mentor for a younger person within the past year
- Has written at least one letter or e-mail to an elected official in the last year about a concern
- Is a member of a civic organization, trade union, religious organization, or social-change organization
- Contributes at least $25 yearly to a nonprofit organization doing good in the world
- Serves to help meet a community need, e.g. childcare, eldercare, food pantry
- Keeps learning to understand the current social, political, and economic situation
- Other?

11
YouthBuild Graduate Leaders Network

GRADUATES AS LEADERS

YouthBuild has helped develop thousands of young leaders over the last three decades. They are parents, union leaders, teachers, pastors, elected officials, business owners, community activists, home owners, social workers, and YouthBuild directors. They are working on issues like immigration rights, prison reform, parent support, crime prevention, climate change, student debt, home foreclosures, healthy eating, political campaigns, AIDS/HIV education, community service, and much more.

We are in touch with some of them, but we know little to nothing about the vast majority who are simply living responsible lives contributing to their communities. Once in a while, a graduate will write us out of the blue, like the letter Dorothy Stoneman received from José, who was a graduate of the Youth Action Program YouthBuild in the early 1980s. He said that after graduating, he tried college, then moved out of state, got married, had three children, and is now the deputy sheriff of a town in Pennsylvania. He was just writing to thank anyone who was still at the Youth Action Program for setting him on the right path. He is forever grateful.

Quite often, we get a letter or call from a graduate who graduated 10 or 15 years ago who says that he or she has been out in the wider world doing well but that nothing compares with the positive energy, community service, and leadership experiences in YouthBuild. The question is how can they plug back in? One said that his wife told him to quit reminiscing about YouthBuild as the best thing he ever did and to get back involved!

Many local directors and staff receive similar letters or visits from graduates. Then there are the hundreds of graduate leaders that have emerged over the years who are still involved with YouthBuild. In addition to all that local programs do to remain connected with graduates, over the past several decades YouthBuild USA has sustained multiple pathways into leadership for YouthBuild graduates. As of this writing, in 2013, the investment totals over a half million dollars a year in events, speaking opportunities, staff support, scholarships, and direct grants to graduates.

YOUTHBUILD USA 1000 LEADERS NETWORK

YouthBuild USA, mostly through the work of its graduate leadership department, has established the YouthBuild USA 1000 Leaders Network, a membership association aimed at identifying, organizing, and occasionally mobilizing YouthBuild graduate leaders. The network currently engages graduates in the following ways.

The national Young Leaders Council (YLC). This is a group of approximately 25 young leaders, elected by their peers at the annual Conference of Young Leaders in Washington, DC, which is attended by about 120 current students from about 60 YouthBuild programs). They serve three-year terms, meeting twice a year for three days in person and having monthly conference calls. The YLC provides YouthBuild USA with key feedback on policy questions and represents YouthBuild at national forums. Each meeting also gives attention to participants' leadership skills. Many YLC members later serve as staff for the Conference of Young Leaders.

The National Alumni Council (NAC). The NAC is the older graduate group, about 15 in number, elected by their peers at the Alumni Xchange conference. They serve three-year terms and are the guiding force for the graduate network. They meet three times a year for three or four days each in various YouthBuild hub cities (cities for which there are four to six YouthBuild programs within a 90-minute drive) and lead daylong Regional Leadership Gatherings for 80 to 250 current YouthBuild students. In their own meetings, they focus on continued self-development, leadership skill building, policy making for the graduate network, planning the Alumni Xchange, and helping to coordinate various national partnerships and leadership events.

The VOICES Council (Views On Improving Credential & Education Success). These are graduates who are in college or other postsecondary education venues. Meeting twice a year, these student leaders inform YouthBuild USA about the necessary supports and resources students need to successfully transition from a YouthBuild program to postsecondary education. VOICES members provide input on three key areas: academics, financial aid, and student support services.

The National Speakers Bureau includes YouthBuild graduate leaders who advocate for YouthBuild and highlight their own issues, struggles, and concerns as well as their recommendations on how to rectify these matters. They are called upon to speak at conferences, appear on panels, serve on policy forums, or present workshops. There are currently several hundred members of the Speakers Bureau.

Alumni Xchange. This is a high-energy biannual national gathering of members of the 1000 Leaders Network. It is planned and facilitated by the NAC and attended by 100 to 150 graduate leaders and includes leadership and professional development skills training, networking, and visioning for graduate impact in the world.

Graduates on Staff Project. Over 100 graduates serve as staff at local YouthBuild programs. The Graduates on Staff initiative gathers information about their onboarding process and professional development, offers a forum for them to share learnings and challenges, and provides support and advocacy for their future development.

The Declaration of Inter-Dependence is the policy statement that YouthBuild USA has supported the YLC and NAC to create, first written in 1999, and revised every four years through 2008. It is the best thinking of YouthBuild graduates on the areas critical to their lives: public schools, family supports, community economic development, respect for young people, the criminal justice system, and protecting the planet and our environment.

Six graduate leaders (two each from the YLC, the NAC, and VOICES) are members of the YouthBuild USA Affiliated Network Policy Council, a democratic decision-making structure. These six individuals join six YouthBuild directors and six YouthBuild USA staff to decide policy and direction for the network of affiliated YouthBuild programs.

Five YouthBuild graduates currently serve on the YouthBuild USA Board of Directors.

YouthBuild graduates are on the staff of the graduate leadership department (GLD) at YouthBuild USA, including the director of leadership development. In recent years, a graduate has also served as a VISTA in the GLD.

The National Council of Young Leaders (NCYL) is a recent development that moves beyond YouthBuild to involve young leaders from seven other national networks. It was launched in 2012 as a major voice of opportunity youth and has a well-developed policy document, *Recommendations to Increase Opportunity and Decrease Poverty in America.* These Recommendations can be used as curriculum for current students and as a way to generate conversation about local needs. Local alumni clubs can also sign onto these recommendations. The NCYL grows directly from the graduate work YouthBuild USA has sustained over the years, and promises to have increasing impact.

Opportunities and supports. YouthBuild USA also:

- Runs a YouthBuild AmeriCorps initiative through which over 3,000 students annually earn an AmeriCorps Education Award

- Funds an Asset Trust fund that gives about $70,000 a year in gifts to graduates to see them through a rough financial patch in their lives or to provide opportunities

- Manages the Helene D. Stoneman Scholarships, which selects 35 to 40 YouthBuild college students per year for $2,000 scholarships

- Coordinates the placement of graduates into their next step in leadership development into other national organizations including VISTA, National Civilian Conservation Corps, Public Allies, and Year Up.

GRADUATE LEADERSHIP—THE NEXT PHASE

With the growing numbers, sophistication, and accomplishments of YouthBuild graduate leaders, the sky is the limit for their future influence and impact. Below are some ideas that have been put forward by graduates and staff that are exciting prospects.

Individual development ideas
There are increasing numbers of YouthBuild graduates and staff willing and able to teach other graduates skills that graduates are requesting, such as how to write proposals and do fundraising, public speaking and presentation, workshop design and facilitation, healthy living

and stress management, peer counseling, and developing healthy relationships.

Fellowship support networks

Groups of like-minded graduates can organize themselves around interests to provide encouragement, support, contacts, and good ideas. Examples includes topics like social change and organizing, spirituality, healthy eating and lifestyle, music producing, effective parenting, and creation of new nonprofits serving the community. Meetings can be either virtual or face-to-face.

Professional development and business ideas

Graduate consulting company. One idea is to develop a graduate-training and consulting company. There are many graduates who are superb trainers and facilitators and could bring a wealth of Youth-Build perspective to programs. By forming a company, they would organize them into a consulting corps and develop other graduates through training in workshop design, facilitation skills, and coaching methods. Graduates can provide technical assistance and training to YouthBuild programs on leadership development, policy committees, youth development, program culture and discipline, diversity, and more, depending on their growing expertise and the needs of the sites. This could provide leadership opportunities and income for the graduates and invaluable assistance to programs.

Graduate construction companies. A second promising venture is the formation of local graduate construction companies. This has been successfully done in a handful of places, but with training and seed money, it could be a natural extension of the YouthBuild experience for more and more graduates. The green-building sector will soon be clamoring for skilled workers. Why not get program-run or graduate-run companies in place to take advantage of this emerging field. One variation that is now being tried is the development of a solar-window installation business that will hire graduates and produce revenue for the programs.

Music production. One graduate has his own music-production company and wants to produce the positive message music of YouthBuild graduates, to showcase their amazing talent and creativity. This could catapult the visibility of YouthBuild, be a source of inspiration to young listeners, and provide some income to the artists.

Graduates-as-YouthBuild-directors training track. Another idea is to create a systematic training and development pathway for interested and talented graduates who aspire to be YouthBuild program managers and directors. This could be a joint project between local YouthBuild programs and YouthBuild USA. As of this writing, at least five YouthBuild graduates are or have been YouthBuild directors or managers. The pace of this growth process should be deliberately accelerated so that there are scores of graduate YouthBuild directors by 2020. Several graduates are currently leading efforts to create new YouthBuild programs.

Graduate leadership in the YouthBuild network

In addition to several of the ideas listed above, there are various ways graduates can help build the YouthBuild network. Many graduates are already filling such roles.

Assist with recruiting and orientation. YouthBuild graduates can be among the best recruiters of new students. Especially if they have caught the leadership bug during their own time as students, they would have an interest in building up the leadership corps coming through YouthBuild. Graduates have also proven themselves to be valuable role models and teachers during the Mental Toughness orientation.

Start or support an alumni club. As noted in chapter 10 (Graduate Resources), many sites struggle to maintain contact with graduates. Supporting a graduate leader to keep in touch with graduates can help. Some graduates can and have gathered other graduates together on their own, in their homes, but they also want to be welcomed in the program. Program support makes a big difference.

Mentor young people. An obvious role for graduate leaders is to be mentors for younger people coming behind them, especially Youth-Build students.

Build statewide leadership pathways. Through funding secured from the Knight Foundation, by YouthBuild USA, is now replicating at the state level some of the leadership platforms that exist at the national level. Elements of this process include:

- A state-based coordinator

- Statewide speakers bureau

- State alumni exchange (AX), similar to the national AX

- State alumni council, or STAC, elected at the state AX, similar to the National Alumni Council (NAC)

- The coordinator, with assistance from the STAC, will coordinate graduate leadership work in that state:

  - Developing local alumni clubs

  - Supporting graduates on staffs

  - Planning state advocacy efforts in conjunction with the state YouthBuild coalition

  - Offering TA and training to programs

  - Maintaining a robust social-media networking platforms to link graduates with each other

  - Developing state-based policy papers focused first on improving the education system and the criminal justice system—two systems that have failed YouthBuild young people and about which they have important recommendations

Social justice and movement building

Increasingly, YouthBuild graduate leaders are positioned to play major leadership roles beyond YouthBuild. Again, the sky is the limit. Here are some beginning ideas that have been proposed by graduates and staff. Note that each of them would require focused resources and attention.

Develop a young-adult equivalent of AARP. AARP, the American Association of Retired People, has 37 million members. It is the largest, most powerful advocacy group in the country. They make sure that Medicare and Social Security are not touched by cost-cutting politicians. Near the other end of the age spectrum, young adults—across class and race—have their own issues, such as college access and affordability, college debt, police abuse and mass incarceration, affordable housing, access to child care, and poor job prospects or low wages after graduation. Therefore, could YouthBuild graduates, working with young leaders from other groups and constituencies, organize a young-adult association that lobbied and spoke out about their issues? This would need to be separate from YouthBuild and YouthBuild USA but would incorporate the core values of YouthBuild—love, responsibility, knowledge, community, service, and leadership. If this could be done, such an association could be a new force in politics. Graduates have floated the name American Association of Young Adults, AAYA.

Trainers for other social-justice organizations. Skilled YouthBuild graduate leaders could become training facilitators who would deliver the workshops of other change organizations like United for a Fair Economy, Mobilize.org, New Economics Institute, Opportunity Nation, National Council of La Raza, Green for All, Rebuild the Dream, ACLU, Training for Change, NAACP, and others. One project that has begun involves the development of a powerful multimedia presentation about climate change, global warming, and environmental justice that YouthBuild graduates would deliver in their own communities—a kind of *An Inconvenient Truth* for the hood. Another benefit would be that these graduates can also provide these trainings for the YouthBuild network.

Young People's TV. Some graduates have expressed interest in learning how to create and host their own public-access TV shows with, by, and about young people. This could be an avenue for learning, networking, organizing, and recruiting other young leaders.

National Council of Young Leaders. As mentioned earlier, the National Council of Young Leaders (NCYL) is a new policy group positioned to sit at many influential tables representing the voice of opportunity youth. Individual graduates and the state and national graduate councils can find ways to support the recommendations and legislative campaigns of the NCYL. YouthBuild graduates can consider the NCYL as speaking for them at the national level, can be in dialogue with NCYL members, and can communicate with young leaders from the other organizations represented on the council.

Public service and policy training program. Increasingly, YouthBuild graduates are serving on influential boards and policy forums. To multiply those numbers and better equip graduates for these roles, we could develop a training and coaching program for senior graduate leaders who are oriented towards public service.

Electoral politics. Some graduates are running for elected office at the local level—there are graduates who have run for school committee, planning board, district leader, library council, county commission, and more. This will increase as graduates' work and family lives become stable and they have the space to get involved in electoral politics. YouthBuild USA can provide training, expertise, and networking platforms on how to run campaigns or position oneself to run. Youth-Build candidates could be supported by the young-adult AARP!

Youth Leadership "University." In 1992 I wrote a concept paper for a residential-leadership program for outstanding leaders who are graduates of YouthBuild (and perhaps from the youth divisions of other national organizations like the National Council of La Raza, The Corps Network, Year Up, NAACP, ASPIRA, Public Allies, National Urban League, etc.). We did not get it funded then but it is still an idea worth pursuing. This would give young leaders additional support for taking their leadership to another level. As in college, the young people would live together. They would study leadership theories, the histories of social movements, and non-violent strategies. They would learn community organizing and advocacy skills. They would do deep personal and professional work on the issues of cultural diversity. They would volunteer in a local community organization to learn in the trenches. They would learn how to live together, solve conflicts, and create community—a yearlong learning experience in the group dynamics of forming, norming, storming, and performing. They would envision new forms of social, economic, and political organization, and strategize for making the vision real. A visionary leader plus major funding, infrastructure, and groundwork would be needed to realize this vision, but it is worth keeping as a possibility.

International youth exchanges. As in the United States, many outstanding young leaders are emerging from the YouthBuild programs in other countries. We could reap enormous benefits from getting these leaders together. We should raise the funding to organize international exchanges among these young leaders—exchanges that would combine work and service projects, cultural learning, leadership development, global consciousness expansion, and personal connections across borders. One graduate has suggested that an outgrowth of such international exchanges among YouthBuild graduates is that they come to be a resource for global entities like UNESCO or the Clinton Global Initiative, sharing their ideas and experiences for solving vexing problems affecting young people around the globe.

Direct action. Our economic and political systems need fundamental change. Many graduates have participated in direct-action campaigns in their local communities on issues like immigration, criminal-justice reform, union organizing, voting rights, and so on. There are limitless opportunities for graduates to help bring about a society whose aim is the well-being of all people, all communities, and the planet. Many of these actions and campaigns will need to take place outside of Youth-Build because of YouthBuild's funding and political constraints.

One can begin to get very excited about the emergence of YouthBuild graduates as change agents, policy makers, and elected officials. It is already happening. Graduates are and will be doing much more of this on their own in any case. The relevant question for YouthBuild programs is to what extent could graduates be organized, coordinated, and united into a more powerful force for good by deliberate training, development, strategy, support, positioning, funding, and communication? This will need to be include graduates at the core, but can be supported by and in some cases led by YouthBuild USA, the National Alumni Council, the YouthBuild USA Affiliated Network, and local YouthBuild programs. Indeed, the sky's the limit!

12

YouthBuild's North Star: Answering a Call

outhBuild is one of the most successful national youth, leadership, and community-development programs in the country. Our work is widely acclaimed, deeply researched, even used as case studies in graduate schools. In October of 2013 we celebrated YouthBuild's 35th anniversary, during which we touted many significant accomplishments as of that date:

- 120,000 graduates have built 22,000 units of affordable housing.

- Tens of thousands of young people from low-income backgrounds have transformed their lives and become productive citizens and community leaders.

- 273 programs are operating in the poorest communities of the United States.

- 102 YouthBuild programs exist in 14 other countries, each led by dedicated entrepreneurial local leaders.

We have also maintained an annual federal-budget line item totaling $1.3 billion since 1994, developed a strong partnership with the federal government, and built an outstanding service delivery system with training, technical assistance, and funding. In all these ways YouthBuild is an undeniable success. We are grateful and happy for the impact YouthBuild has had.

But there is a heartbreaking underbelly to all this. In the 35 years since we began in East Harlem in 1978, despite the tireless work of thousands of YouthBuild staff, the perseverance of young people who find their way to YouthBuild, the massive investments from public and private sources, the conditions in many YouthBuild communities have gotten worse. Income inequality is greater. Poverty is deep. Despair is strong. School dropout rates are steep. Incarceration is massive. Unemployment is staggering. Opportunity has narrowed. Addiction is rampant. Gang activity is generations old. Additionally, in the wider world, every day we increasingly see signs that the political system is broken, people are suffering, and the planet is imperiled.

The good news is that YouthBuild is sitting on a huge potential positive force to help turn these conditions around, namely the ten thousand young adults that enter our YouthBuild programs each year, and the tens of thousands of graduates in recent years. But this potential largely evaporates after the program cycle. In my opinion, there are three main reasons for this that I have tried to address in this book. As a network of programs:

- We have not viewed the promotion and sustaining of young leaders as fundamental to our work, as a core deliverable. Thus, we have not designed our programs to maximize leadership development, so most young people leave with insufficient tools, training, networks, or pathways to maximize their leadership. Certainly, most graduates make some gains, and many figure out how to play a leadership role in their lives. But compared to what is possible, there is a huge miss.

- Secondly, we have not adequately developed the capacity to assist young people to liberate themselves from the grip of their inner pain, negative habits, and internalized oppression. Thus, ongoing "drama," self-destructive behavior, and repetition of unworkable habits continue to devour their life energies, keeping many of them focused on emotional or economic survival rather than flourishing and leading.

- And, thirdly, neither programs nor graduates nor YouthBuild USA have created sustainable ways to engage, organize, support, and mobilize graduates for collective social-justice efforts once they leave the full-time program. Thus, the potential force for good is drained away, lost. The time and investment made during the program year is not captured, and the gains made by individual young people can be easily wiped away by society's failures.

YouthBuild is not alone in facing the ugly truth that some things have gotten worse in low-income communities. Most organizations working on some aspect of alleviating poverty have probably no doubt noticed that overall conditions for low-income people have not improved. The services and opportunities that are provided by Youth-Build and its sister organizations are critically important. Real people need real help with real problems. But providing services alone cannot change the conditions that give rise to the problems we aim to address.

As I recalled in the early parts of this book, from its beginnings, Youth-Build was intended to be a movement-building effort aimed at bringing about what Martin Luther King Jr. called the "beloved community"— where opportunity, fairness, mutual respect, and social harmony prevail. In this movement, young people raised in poverty are a huge potential force for liberation. That is why YouthBuild has focused on the need for leadership development. Certainly we must provide services and opportunities along the way. But YouthBuild offers young people the opportunity to transform their own lives by being actors and leaders, by serving the community through building affordable housing and other service projects, by advancing their education, and by creating a positive, healthy peer community. This approach moves them out of being just clients getting services and points them in the direction of being change agents, as they emerge from their own individual survival stance.

Climate change, immigration, population growth, consumerism, resource depletion, poverty, unemployment, and debt are huge worldwide forces that impact low-income communities hardest. Gains made by people that our well-intentioned and successful nonprofit organizations serve can be wiped away by these larger forces. The point that has been repeated in this book is the need to marry the social-service work we do with a more intentional, purposeful, and intensive social change focus. This is YouthBuild's North Star.

Here is a brief summary of the main points of this book.

There is a need for a global movement for social transformation. Given world conditions, it is time to collectively develop a moral, positive, nonviolent engaged citizenry to protect the planet, pursue the peace, empower the people, and promote prosperity.

There is a need for young leaders from low-income communities. Given the state of the world, there is a growing time-urgency for leaders to emerge from low-income backgrounds. The solutions will not come from government or corporations alone as they are currently structured. People from low-income communities who are most affected by climate change, unemployment, poor education, a skewed police and criminal justice system, need to be at the table. This includes young people. Indeed, as we noted in the chapter on leadership development (chapter 6), young people have been the actual front-line force in the great social and political transformations of the last hundred years.

YouthBuild has a potential force for good. In YouthBuild, we have seen that many young people are capable and want to be part of the movement for peace and justice. The 10,000 young people a year in

YouthBuild in the United States, year after year, is an ever-growing and sizable potential force for good, even if only 10 percent of them get the fire in the belly to make a difference.

However, the young people are hampered from becoming that force for the reasons I listed above. Therefore, what I have called for in this book are four strategies to help them realize this potential.

FOUR STRATEGIES FOR BRIGHTENING YOUTHBUILD'S NORTH STAR

1. **Make the development of young leaders an integral, core, essential element and goal of every aspect of YouthBuild.** We will continue to build housing and other tangible community assets, assist young people to gain academic and career certifications, promote postsecondary education and training—all in the context of a positive peer culture. But we can shift to align all of this more deliberately and powerfully with how to develop leadership. Chapters 6 through 10 detail some of the ways to integrate leadership development into every YouthBuild component. What would shift if we made the development of skilled young leaders an essential deliverable or product, equal to every other target we must achieve?

2. **Develop deeper social consciousness.** Set up the YouthBuild programs to help young people understand the issues that affect them and others in a deeper way. Through critical education, project-based learning, intentional exposure to new experiences and broader information, the program can help young people understand root causes of the oppressive conditions they have experienced and seen, envision a healthy and safe world, and learn ways to bring about community and social change. The chapters on leadership and education list many practices.

3. **Deepen healing and personal development.** Leading, learning, and life success are hindered by emotional scarring that Youth-Build young people bring with them. The insecurities, unworkable habits, the repetitive drama form a kind of mental bondage that saps their energy, intelligence, and capacity to lead. Thus, if YouthBuild is to be a more deliberate leadership-development engine, then we are called upon to deepen program capacity to help young people heal and liberate themselves from fear, anger, depression, and lack of self-love. Without deep healing work, the long-range vision of YouthBuild graduates as a collective force for good will be undermined. Chapter 8 (on counseling and healing) offers some practices toward this goal.

4. **Create strong local and national graduate networks.** The tantalizing possibility of YouthBuild graduates playing significant leadership roles in their communities as a mobilized force remains mostly a dream in the absence of strong local graduate networks that encourage, support, train, and incubate graduate-leadership efforts. In order to prevent the loss of the potential force that YouthBuild graduates could be, as a network, we must solve the challenge of developing engaging, robust, growing, multiphased graduate programs and alumni networks. The chapters on graduates, chapters 10 and 11, put forth a vision and recommendations for doing this.

ANSWERING A CALL

Admittedly, these strategies toward positive change are daunting. It is challenging enough to keep the doors open, let alone to take on what is called for in this book, much as we might like to. But, given the world conditions, the stakes are high. The big story of our time is that for the first time in human history, climate change is threatening our very existence. This is added to the ongoing poverty and injustice that already assault low-income people and their communities. I think we are at a crossroads, either breakdown or breakthrough.

In my view, YouthBuild has a big leadership role to play in this big story. Young people's leadership is sorely needed—tens of thousands of skilled, ethical, effective young leaders engaged in tackling the issues of the day. We can turn YouthBuild even more towards being a powerful engine of this leadership development. We can do this if we choose to. Much of this is already happening in YouthBuild.

Some of the shifts I am recommending are new but most are building on and lifting to awareness core elements of the 35 years of collective work that has been awesome, innovative, life-changing, persistent, creative, courageous, detailed, heartbreaking, exhausting, and inspiring. It has been my privilege and honor to work for so long with so many on this noble project. I hope that these recommendations are received in the spirit with which they are written—with gratitude for what we have built together in YouthBuild, optimism about creating the "beloved community", and a fervent hope that we answer the call.

May YouthBuild's North Star shine brightly!

Resources

*T*he following resources were mentioned in the book. They are gathered here by topic with brief descriptions for easy reference. Most are available in the YouthBuild USA Knowledge Bank on the YouthBuild USA website, www.YouthBuild.org. (An easy-to-obtain password may be required.) Other resources have web addresses noted.

PROGRAM CULTURE, DESIGN, AND STAFF BUILDING

1. The best overall guides to developing a comprehensive YouthBuild program are the *YouthBuild Program Handbook,* and *The Youth-Build Affiliated Network Design and Performance Standards*
    - http://northstar.link/youthbuildhandbook
    - http://northstar.link/youthbuildstandards

2. An excellent handbook on each of the five main YouthBuild program components can be found on the YouthBuild USA website.
    - www.YouthBuild.org

3. Dorothy Stoneman wrote several articles on staff-building that are highly recommended. Here are two: "Observations on Power Relationships at a YouthBuild Sites," and "The Art and Challenge of Being a YouthBuild Director."

   ■ http://northstar.link/observations
   ■ http://northstar.link/artandchallenge

For a one-page summary of elements of a well-integrate program, see my article "Recommendations for Building a Transformational Program."

   ■ http://northstar.link/transformational

4. *Blueprint for Democracy* is a basic civics curriculum developed by YouthBuild USA and used by many YouthBuild programs.

   ■ http://northstar.link/blueprint

LEADERSHIP DEVELOPMENT

1. *Leadership Development Handbook,* by Dorothy Stoneman with contributions from John Bell, is a foundational book on the topic. A must read.

   ■ http://northstar.link/youthleadership

2. *Leadership Development at a YouthBuild Program* is the basic implementation handbook, full of practical ideas.

   ■ http://northstar.link/ldatyb

3. For a brief survey of young people contributions to social justice in modern history, see "Contributions of Young People to Social Change," by John Bell.

   ■ http://northstar.link/contributions

4. For guidance on how to create and maintain and effective youth governance committee, see *YouthBuild Policy Committee Handbook,* by John Bell.

   ■ http://northstar.link/policycomhb

5. For those who want to get young people involved in community action or advocacy beyond the YouthBuild program, there is the *Community Leadership Committee Handbook.*

   ■ http://northstar.link/leadershipcomhb

6. YouthBuild USA has developed 23 Leadership Competencies for use in YouthBuild program. The competencies and a sample template for tracking and measuring student achievement of the Leadership Competencies can be found at the links below.

   ■ *Leadership competencies:* http://northstar.link/leadershipcompetencies

   ■ *Templates:* http://northstar.link/leadershiptemplates

7. For descriptions of some effective group-process methods, see the article "Creating Conditions for Good Learning, Thinking, and Decision Making," by John Bell.

   ■ http://northstar.link/creatingconditions

DIVERSITY

1. Issues of diversity are present at every YouthBuild program. See the handbook on *Creating a Diverse Community at YouthBuild,* by John Bell, for ideas on how to use diversity as an organizational asset and learning method.

   ■ http://northstar.link/diversecommunity

2. For an explanation of several aspects of any system of oppression, see "Four Is of Oppression," by John Bell.

   ■ http://northstar.link/fouris

3. For two companion pieces of working on issues of diversity, see "Working On Issues Of Oppression With Young People" and "Eliminating Internalized Oppression," both by John Bell.

   ■ *Issues of Oppression:* http://northstar.link/issuesofoppression

   ■ *Eliminating Internalized Oppression:* http://northstar.link/internalizedoppression

4. To be successful in our work with young people, we must understand a particular condition of youth: that young people are often mistreated and disrespected simply because they are young. *Adultism* refers to behaviors and attitudes based on the assumption that adults are better than young people, and entitled to act upon young people without their agreement. For more, read "Understanding Adultism," by John Bell.
   - http://northstar.link/adultism

EDUCATION

1. The basic information about education practice in YouthBuild can be found in the *Education at a YouthBuild Program* handbook.
   - http://ybhandbooks.org/files/tools/
     Education-at-a-YouthBuild-Program-2013.pdf

2. CASEL is an organization founded by Daniel Goleman, who wrote the best-selling book *Emotional Intelligence*. CASEL is warehouse of great information about the whole field of social and emotional learning, which focuses on the soft-skill and heart-centered side of education.
   - www.casel.org

3. Mockingbird Education is a well-developed, integrated approach to teaching, learning, and curricula development which has been successfully adapted by many YouthBuild programs.
   - www.mockingbirdeducation.net

4. The leadership curriculum outlined in the *Youth Leadership Development Handbook*, by Dorothy Stoneman, is fairly comprehensive, covering such topics as big social change movements, theories of oppression, and dealing with emotional hurts.
   - http://northstar.link/youthleadership

5. For good information on politics and economics to help young people build a base of knowledge, see **United for a Fair Economy,** and the **Center for Popular Economics,** both located in Massachusetts. They have curricula, trainings, and deep working knowledge of the issues which poor and working people face, all of which can be adapted to YouthBuild populations. The **California YouthBuild Charter School** has developed a social justice-oriented curriculum called the *ACE Manual,* developed by YouthBuild teachers, that is well worth checking out.
   - www.faireconomy.org
   - www.populareconomics.org
   - www.youthbuildcharter.org
   - http://northstar.link/acemanual

6. Use *Blueprint for Democracy,* an excellent basic civics curriculum developed by YouthBuild USA and used to good end by many YouthBuild programs. This curriculum, in part, makes a strong case for the importance of voting and taking part in the electoral process as a means of affecting change.
   - http://northstar.link/blueprint

7. Have students read and discuss the *Declaration of Inter-Dependence,* created by YouthBuild National Alumni Council and Young Leaders Council. It a policy paper on six critical issues that affect the lives and communities of YouthBuild young people.
   - http://northstar.link/declaration

8. YouthBuild USA has convened the National Council of Young Leaders, on which sit representatives from various national youth organizations. The council has produced its set of *Recommendations for Increasing Opportunity and Decreasing Poverty.*
   - http://northstar.link/ncylrecommendations

9. *World Peace and Other 4th-Grade Achievements*, by John Hunter, is an inspiring account of respect for the ability of young people to think deeply and solve major societal problems cooperatively.
   - www.worldpeacegame.org/the-book

10. *How Children Succeed*, by Paul Tough, is an excellent survey of research and practice of resilience, character development, and social-emotional learning. Highly relevant for YouthBuild.
    - www.paultough.com/the-books/how-children-succeed

COUNSELING AND HEALING

1. *Counseling and Case Management at a YouthBuild Program*
   ■ http://northstar.link/counselingatyb

2. For over 40 years, Dorothy Stoneman and John Bell have benefited immensely from the theory and practice of Re-evaluation Counseling. It is a method of peer counseling that emphasizes skillful listening, the release of feelings, and the recovery of our full intelligence and capacities out from under accumulated hurts and traumas of life. There are certified teachers located in many YouthBuild cities.
   ■ www.rc.org

3. For a brief introduction to the Re-evaluation Counseling approach to human nature, the effects of hurt and trauma, and the recovery process, adapted to the YouthBuild context, see the article "The Process of Emotional Healing," by John Bell.
   ■ http://northstar.link/emotionalhealing

4. A printable version of the appreciation chart at the end of Chapter 7 is available for download.
   ■ http://northstar.link/appreciationchart

5. *Power Source®* is an excellent resource that can help young people talk about troubling issues in their lives. The book alternates between short stories written by young people and strategies for handling those issues. Highly recommended by many YouthBuild programs. Comes with a well-designed teacher's manual.
   ■ www.lionheart.org

6. Restorative Justice is a growing alternative to the punitive justice model. It engages the "wrongdoer" and the "wronged" in a process of restoring ruptured relationships. This methodology is being using in an increasing number of YouthBuild programs with excellent results.
   ■ www.iirp.edu

7. *Nonviolent Communication* is a theory and practice that helps people talk through conflict without resorting to violence. Effective life-long tool, with many practical applications. Certified instructors available in many locations.

   ■ www.cnvc.org

8. TruThought® is a cognitive behavioral method that helps people examine their thought processes that lead to positive or ineffective behavior. Used by several YouthBuild programs.

   ■ www.truthought.com

9. Developing healthy relationships is a central need for YouthBuild young people. In some ways, it is where life is most vividly lived, with all the joys and the drama. YouthBuild USA has sponsored a training in a 16-week relationships curriculum called *Love Notes*. It has been successfully and enthusiastically implemented at about 20 YouthBuild programs. Curriculum is available at the Dibble Institute's website. Training is available through YouthBuild USA.

   ■ www.dibbleinstitute.org

10. *Choice Theory*, derived from the work of William Glasser PhD, emphasizes behavior change, personal responsibility and consequences, and taking complete charge of oneself.

    ■ wglasser.com/the-glasser-approach/choice-theory

CONSTRUCTION

1. The basics of implementing a successful construction component can be found in *Construction Training at a YouthBuild Program.* Excellent material for integrating vocational education and leadership can be found in the multivolume curriculum called *Working Hands, Working Minds;* all volumes are available through the YouthBuild USA website.

   ■ http://northstar.link/constructionatyb
   ■ http://northstar.link/workinghands

2. For implementation of green construction at YouthBuild, see *Shades of Green.*
   - www.ybshadesofgreen.org

GRADUATE RESOURCES

1. Valuable guidelines for implementing a graduate program can be found in *Counseling and Case Management at a YouthBuild Program.*
   - http://northstar.link/counselingatyb

2. For ideas on supporting graduates in postsecondary education and training, see "Creating Graduate Support Systems."
   - http://northstar.link/gradsupport

RELEVANT RESEARCH STUDIES

1. Conducted by researchers at Brandeis and Temple Universities, *Life After YouthBuild* is a study on the lasting effects of YouthBuild on the lives of nearly 900 YouthBuild graduates, from one to seven years after graduation.
   - http://northstar.link/lifeafteryb

2. *Pathways in Leadership: A Study of YouthBuild Graduates,* by CIRCLE at Tufts University, summarizes the impressive results of sustained investment in youth leadership skill development of Youth-Build graduate leaders.
   - http://northstar.link/pathways

3. For a list of skills sought by employers and postsecondary institutions as determined by the U.S. Department of Labor, see the SCANS report.
   - http://northstar.link/scans

4. For a summary of the process of youth transformation in Youth-Build, see Dr. Ronald Ferguson's piece "The Process of Personal Transformation at YouthBuild."
   - http://northstar.link/personaltransformation

5. The Ford Foundation funded the Center for Innovation study of 20 youth organizations, showing youth in leadership programs made more gains in youth development than in traditional youth program.
   - http://www.theinnovationcenter.org/files/Lessons_in_Leadership_exec.pdf

6. For information on the link between policy committees and higher program outcomes, see a study conducted by Social Policy Research Associates (SPRA) called "Evaluation of the YouthBuild Youth Offender Grants."
   - http://northstar.link/evalyogrants

53418321R00139

Made in the USA
Middletown, DE
27 November 2017